THE

INTERNATIONAL

SPACE STATION

TITLES IN THE BUILDING HISTORY SERIES INCLUDE:

THE

INTERNATIONAL

SPACE STATION

by Marcia Amidon Lüsted

LUCENT BOOKS

An imprint of Thomson Gale, a part of The Thomson Corporation

THOMSON
✳
™
GALE

Detroit • New York • San Francisco • San Diego • New Haven, Conn.
Waterville, Maine • London • Munich

THOMSON

——————✦——————™

GALE

For more information, contact
Lucent Books
27500 Drake Rd.
Farmington Hills, MI 48331-3535
Or you can visit our Internet site at http://www.gale.com

LIBRARY OF CONGRESS CATALOGING-IN-PUBLICATION DATA

Lüsted, Marcia Amidon.
    The International Space Station / by Marcia Amidon Lüsted.
        p. cm. — (Building history series)
Includes bibliographical references and index.
ISBN 1-59018-666-4 (hardcover : alk. paper)
1. International Space Station—Juvenile literature. I. Title. II. Series.
TL797.15.L87 2005
629.44'2—dc22

                                                                                    2005001519

Printed in the United States of America

T 27643

CONTENTS

FOREWORD

Throughout history, as civilizations have evolved and prospered, each has produced unique buildings and architectural styles. Combining the need for both utility and artistic expression, a society's buildings, particularly its large-scale public structures, often reflect the individual character traits that distinguish it from other societies. In a very real sense, then, buildings express a society's values and unique characteristics in tangible form. As scholar Anita Abramovitz comments in her book *People and Spaces*, "Our ways of living and thinking—our habits, needs, fear of enemies, aspirations, materialistic concerns, and religious beliefs—have influenced the kinds of spaces that we build and that later surround and include us."

That specific types and styles of structures constitute an outward expression of the spirit of an individual people or era can be seen in the diverse ways that various societies have built palaces, fortresses, tombs, churches, government buildings, sports arenas, public works, and other such monuments. The ancient Greeks, for instance, were a supremely rational people who originated Western philosophy and science, including the atomic theory and the realization that the Earth is a sphere. Their public buildings, epitomized by Athens's magnificent Parthenon temple, were equally rational, emphasizing order, harmony, reason, and above all, restraint.

By contrast, the Romans, who conquered and absorbed the Greek lands, were a highly practical people preoccupied with acquiring and wielding power over others. The Romans greatly admired and readily copied elements of Greek architecture, but modified and adapted them to their own needs. "Roman genius was called into action by the enormous practical needs of a world empire," wrote historian Edith Hamilton. "Rome met them magnificently. Buildings tremendous, indomitable, amphitheaters where eighty thousand could watch a spectacle, baths where three thousand could bathe at the same time."

In medieval Europe, God heavily influenced and motivated the people, and religion permeated all aspects of society, molding people's worldviews and guiding their everyday actions. That spiritual mind-set is reflected in the most important medieval structure—the Gothic cathedral—which, in a sense, was a model of heavenly cities. As scholar Anne Fremantle so elegantly phrases it, the cathedrals were "harmonious elevations of stone and glass reaching up to heaven to seek and receive the light [of God]."

Our more secular modern age, in contrast, is driven by the realities of a global economy, advanced technology, and mass communications. Responding to the needs of international trade and the growth of cities housing millions of people, today's builders construct engineering marvels, among them towering skyscrapers of steel and glass, mammoth marine canals, and huge and elaborate rapid transit systems, all of which would have left their ancestors, even the Romans, awestruck.

In examining some of humanity's greatest edifices, Lucent Books' Building History series recognizes this close relationship between a society's historical character and its buildings. Each volume in the series begins with a historical sketch of the people who erected the edifice, exploring their major achievements as well as the beliefs, customs, and societal needs that dictated the variety, functions, and styles of their buildings. A detailed explanation of how the selected structure was conceived, designed, and built, to the extent that this information is known, makes up the majority of the volume.

Each volume in the Lucent Building History series also includes several special features that are useful tools for additional research. A chronology of important dates gives students an overview, at a glance, of the evolution and use of the structure described. Sidebars create a broader context by adding further details on some of the architects, engineers, and construction tools, materials, and methods that made each structure a reality, as well as the social, political, and/or religious leaders and movements that inspired its creation. Useful maps help the reader locate the nations, cities, streets, and individual structures mentioned in the text; and numerous diagrams and pictures illustrate tools and devices that bring to life various stages of construction. Finally, each volume contains two bibliographies, one for student research, the other listing works the author consulted in compiling the book.

Taken as a whole, these volumes, covering diverse ancient and modern structures, constitute not only a valuable research tool, but also a tribute to the human spirit, a fascinating exploration of the dreams, skills, ingenuity, and dogged determination of the great peoples who shaped history.

IMPORTANT DATES IN THE CONSTRUCTION OF THE INTERNATIONAL SPACE STATION

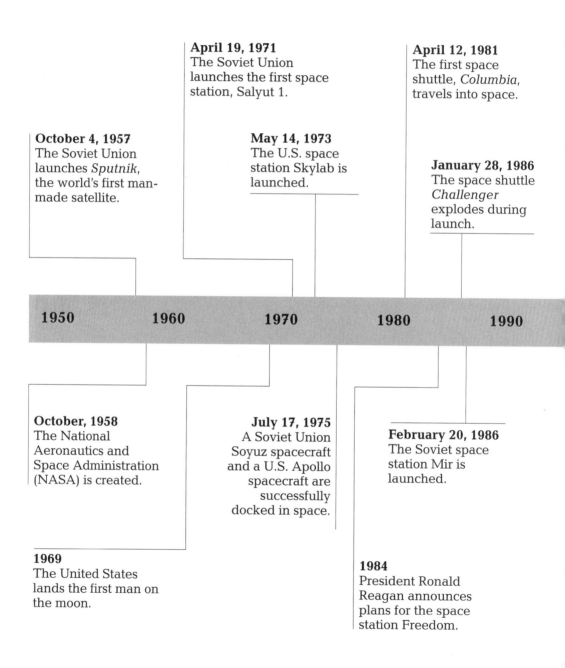

April 19, 1971
The Soviet Union launches the first space station, Salyut 1.

April 12, 1981
The first space shuttle, *Columbia*, travels into space.

October 4, 1957
The Soviet Union launches *Sputnik*, the world's first man-made satellite.

May 14, 1973
The U.S. space station Skylab is launched.

January 28, 1986
The space shuttle *Challenger* explodes during launch.

| 1950 | 1960 | 1970 | 1980 | 1990 |

October, 1958
The National Aeronautics and Space Administration (NASA) is created.

July 17, 1975
A Soviet Union Soyuz spacecraft and a U.S. Apollo spacecraft are successfully docked in space.

February 20, 1986
The Soviet space station Mir is launched.

1969
The United States lands the first man on the moon.

1984
President Ronald Reagan announces plans for the space station Freedom.

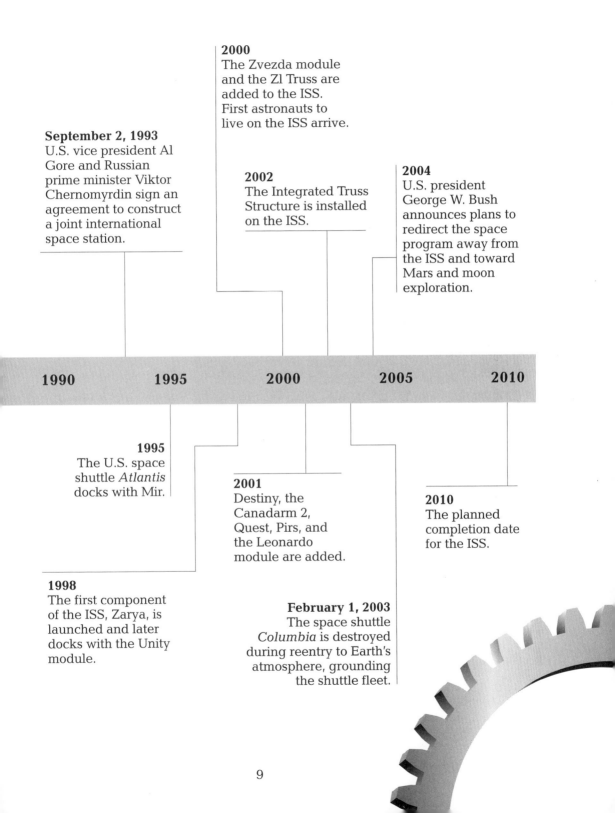

September 2, 1993
U.S. vice president Al Gore and Russian prime minister Viktor Chernomyrdin sign an agreement to construct a joint international space station.

2000
The Zvezda module and the Zl Truss are added to the ISS. First astronauts to live on the ISS arrive.

2002
The Integrated Truss Structure is installed on the ISS.

2004
U.S. president George W. Bush announces plans to redirect the space program away from the ISS and toward Mars and moon exploration.

1990   1995   2000   2005   2010

1995
The U.S. space shuttle *Atlantis* docks with Mir.

2001
Destiny, the Canadarm 2, Quest, Pirs, and the Leonardo module are added.

2010
The planned completion date for the ISS.

1998
The first component of the ISS, Zarya, is launched and later docks with the Unity module.

February 1, 2003
The space shuttle *Columbia* is destroyed during reentry to Earth's atmosphere, grounding the shuttle fleet.

INTRODUCTION

A JOINT VENTURE

In November 1998 the first component of what would become the International Space Station (also known as the ISS) was launched into orbit, creating the first building block of a joint space venture unlike anything that had taken place before in space exploration. Although the ISS would utilize the very newest in space technology, the idea of a space station in orbit around the earth was not a new one.

As early as 1687, Sir Isaac Newton was developing his laws of motion, scientific principles that would later be used to explain how an object could be kept in orbit in space. If an object could be launched into space with enough force and then released, it could remain in orbit because the force of gravity would bend its path around the earth.

Other people also explored the idea of humans inhabiting a structure in space. In 1869 a New England clergyman and writer named Edward Hale published a short story called "The Brick Moon." In this story, several men decide to launch a moon made out of brick into the sky to orbit the earth, using a system of flywheels:

> When the Brick Moon was finished, and all was ready, it should be . . . snapped upward, as a drop of water from a grindstone. Upward and northward it would rise, therefore, till it had passed the axis of the world. It would, of course, feel the earth's attraction all the time, which would bend its flight gently, but still it would leave the world more and more behind. The curve it is now on will forever clear the world; and . . . will forever revolve, in its obedient orbit, the BRICK MOON.[1]

In this story, the brick moon, which is intended to act as a navigational aid for ships, is accidentally launched with people aboard, creating a habitat in space.

Even though it was a science fiction story, "The Brick Moon" illustrates that people had already begun to reach toward space as a

place to explore and possibly colonize. It was not until 1911, however, that Konstantin Tsiolkovsky, a Russian schoolteacher who was
fascinated with space travel and Newton's laws of motion, actually
formulated a design for a large habitation in space. His first magazine article, published in 1903, talked about a future in which rockets and satellites were used in space. According to Peter Bond in
The Continuing Story of the International Space Station:

> Once [Tsiolkovsky] became aware of the potential of rocket
> power, it only required a small leap of his imagination to

*In this illustration from Edward Hale's short story "The Brick Moon," humans
inhabit a man-made satellite orbiting Earth. People began dreaming of space
exploration hundreds of years before it became a possibility.*

In 1952 German scientist Wernher von Braun conceptualized a space station that featured a giant wheel that would rotate to create artificial gravity.

consider the deployment of larger, human-occupied structures in low-Earth orbit, and in 1911 he began to think about space stations. To Tsiolkovsky, it was patently clear that humanity's destiny lay far beyond Earth's cradle . . . [2]

Of course, the construction of a space station could not happen without the means for traveling in space. Space travel took a step closer to becoming a reality in 1926, when an American named Robert Goddard successfully launched a small liquid-fueled rocket 184 feet (56.08m) into the air.

As World War II unfolded, a German man named Wernher von Braun was also making progress with rocket research. Von Braun and a group of scientists were attempting to design a ballistic missile (a missile designed to be launched into high altitudes before coming down on a distant target), while also trying to create a rocket that could reach space. As the war turned against Germany, von Braun and his men surrendered to U.S.

forces and were sent to Huntsville, Alabama, where they continued to do research into rocket travel.

Von Braun became a celebrity of sorts as he continued to build and test successful rockets, but he was also interested in the colonization of space. In an article that appeared in *Collier's* magazine early in 1952, von Braun wrote:

> Within the next 10 or 15 years, the Earth will have a new companion in the skies, a man-made satellite that could either be the greatest force for peace ever devised, or one of the most terrible weapons of war—depending on who makes and controls it. . . . Development of the space station is as inevitable as the rising of the Sun; man has already poked his nose into space and he is not likely to pull it back.[3]

Von Braun described his design for a space station, a huge 250-foot-wide wheel made of reinforced nylon, rotating to create artificial gravity, and containing three decks for living space, communications, weather forecasting, and military purposes. This conception of a space station was the basis for the station in the classic 1968 science fiction movie *2001: A Space Odyssey.* Von Braun's ideas were also presented to the public in three Walt Disney television shows, "Man in Space" (1955), "Man and the Moon" (1955), and "Mars and Beyond" (1957). These shows depicted space travel and space living as an inevitable result of America's supreme technology.

Von Braun was ahead of his time regarding the creation of a space station that could bring cooperation and peace to the countries of the world; it would be many, many years before the ISS would even begin to exist. According to Bond: "The history of the International Space Station is one of the longest running sagas of modern times—a story that covers more than three decades of political intrigue, financial bungling and duplicity, technological wizardry, human courage, and dreams of a brighter future."[4]

The story of the International Space Station begins with the politics of the Cold War, a period after World War II when the United States and the Soviet Union were involved in continuous hostility and lived under the constant threat of nuclear war. During the Cold War a space station was considered a defense weapon rather than a scientific endeavor, but the ISS would turn out to be a project that united two superpowers as never before.

1

THE FIRST
SPACE STATIONS

In the political climate of the 1950s, the Cold War between the United States and the Soviet Union created an atmosphere of distrust. The two nations were striving for military superiority and technical dominance over each other, and part of this competition was a race to develop space technology. These two superpowers competed to see who would be first in space exploration, building several rockets and space stations that would ultimately bring them together in building the International Space Station.

THE WORLD'S FIRST SATELLITE

As early as 1955 the United States announced its intention to launch a man-made satellite (a device designed to be launched into orbit around the earth) into space, but the Soviet Union was far ahead in its ability to make this idea a reality. On October 4, 1957, a small metal globe named *Sputnik* was launched into space by a Soviet rocket. The United States was unaware of this major step in space exploration until the beeping signals sent by *Sputnik*, which could be heard on regular radios, alerted the U.S. space program to what had occurred. It was a blow to the United States to have the Soviets beat them into space, both in terms of developing technology and possibly being able to use this technology for military purposes:

> News that Russia had launched an earth satellite prompted several Senators to demand an investigation of whether the U.S. government was lagging in development of long-range missiles. Senator Stuart Symington (D, Missouri) said that if Russia's "now known superiority over the U.S. develops into a supremacy, the position of the free world will be critical." Senator Henry M. Jackson (D, Washington) called Russia's launching of the

14

satellite a "devastating blow to the prestige of the U.S. as the leader in the scientific and technical world." Senator Alexander Wiley (R, Wisconsin) appraised the Soviets' earth-satellite exploit as "nothing to worry us but something to tell us to keep on our toes."[5]

The launch of *Sputnik* forced the United States to accelerate its own space program, first by launching its own satellite, *Explorer 1*,

A Soviet museum guide displays a replica of Sputnik, *the world's first man-made satellite. The United States launched its own satellite soon after* Sputnik.

early in 1958, followed by the creation of the National Aeronautics and Space Administration (NASA) in October 1958. NASA was vital for uniting all the different space research efforts that were taking place all over the United States under one agency, and one of the first groups transferred to NASA was Wernher von Braun and his colleagues in Huntsville, Alabama.

The United States' first space goals did not include the development of a space station, despite von Braun's dreams of building one. Instead, President John F. Kennedy declared in his 1961 State of the Union address:

> Now it is the time to take longer strides—time for a great new American enterprise—time for this nation to take a clearly leading role in space achievement, which in many ways may hold the key to our future on earth. I believe that this nation should commit itself to achieving the goal, before this decade is out, of landing a man on the moon and returning him safely to the earth. . . . in a very real sense, it will not be one man going to the moon, if we make this judgment affirmatively, it will be an entire nation. It is a most important decision that we make as a nation. But all of you have lived through the last four years and have seen the significance of space and the adventures in space, and no one can predict with certainty what the ultimate meaning will be of mastery of space.[6]

Kennedy's goal was realized when astronauts Neil Armstrong and Edwin "Buzz" Aldrin stepped onto the surface of the moon in 1969, as part of the successful Apollo space program. The United States had briefly bested the Soviet Union in a space race that fostered newer and better technology and more sophisticated space travel. However, the idea of a habitat in space, for both military and scientific purposes, had not died. And again, it would be the Soviet Union that took the first steps toward accomplishing this goal.

THE FIRST HABITAT IN SPACE

On April 19, 1971, the Soviet Union launched the first space station into orbit. Named Salyut 1, the Russian word for "salute," the station was shaped like a cylinder with two pressurized

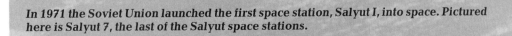

In 1971 the Soviet Union launched the first space station, Salyut I, into space. Pictured here is Salyut 7, the last of the Salyut space stations.

AN APOLLO-SOYUZ HANDSHAKE

While Russian and American cooperation on the ISS signaled a new era of relations between the two countries, their cooperation in space began as early as 1975 with the historic docking of an Apollo spaceship and a Russian Soyuz spaceship. U.S. president Richard Nixon and President Alexei Kosygin of the Soviet Union hoped to bring an end to a decade of breakneck competition between the two space programs.

A small, jointly designed docking adapter was attached to the front of an Apollo capsule in the spot where a lunar module would usually be. This adapter allowed the Apollo ship to dock with the Soyuz ship and included a system for equalizing the pressure between the two ships once docking had taken place.

On July 17, 1975, the two ships docked successfully. The two crews shook hands, entered each other's ships, and shared food and beverages. Not only was it a scientific breakthrough, but many citizens of both countries hoped for a breakthrough in political relations between them as well, as Russians in the streets of the USSR gave bear hugs to foreign visitors. Unfortunately, it would be another twenty years before Russians and Americans would again be this close in space.

This illustration depicts the historic moment in July 1975 when an Apollo spaceship (left) docked with a Soyuz ship.

compartments and an unpressurized service module that held the propulsion system, the "engine" of the station, which allowed it to move in space. Astronauts must have pressurized compartments to live in space, in order to maintain an atmosphere similar to that on Earth and keep a supply of the essential gases their bodies need, which would escape into space in an unpressurized compartment. Air pressure is also needed to enable the astronauts to breathe oxygen.

Salyut 1 contained a research area for scientific experiments and a small space where astronauts lived. Four days after the station was sent into space and reached its orbiting position, three cosmonauts (Russian astronauts) blasted off in a Soyuz rocket and docked with Salyut 1 in space. Although this historic first docking procedure was expected to last for twenty-four hours, to the amazement of the watching world, they remained in place for only five hours. Many years later the Soviet Union admitted that Salyut 1 and the Soyuz transport had been unable to successfully create a pressure seal that would have allowed the astronauts to enter the space station. It was an indication of the highly competitive nature of space exploration as well as the politics of the Cold War that the Soviet Union refused to admit at the time that the docking had been anything less than perfect. Another Soviet crew traveled to Salyut 1 in June 1971, and this crew successfully docked with the space station and lived on board for four weeks, conducting many experiments. Unfortunately, this crew would not be able to share their experiences back on Earth. On June 30 they reentered their spacecraft for the trip home wearing only woolen flight suits, which were usually sufficient for normal reentry. According to Bond:

> As their craft braked to re-enter the upper atmosphere . . . communication with the cosmonauts ceased, but no one on the ground was concerned—radio blackout was a normal consequence as the spacecraft followed its fiery dive through the atmosphere. The parachutes and soft-landing system worked perfectly, but still the hovering helicopter crews were unable to establish a voice link with the returning heroes.

> Then came the shock. As the recovery team opened the Soyuz hatch and peered inside, there was no sign of

In 1973 NASA launched its own space station, Skylab. Six years later, the space station fell out of orbit and reentered the Earth's atmosphere, where most of it burned up.

movement or excited greeting from any of the cosmonauts. Instead, they lay motionless, silent, in their seats. All three were dead. Despite desperate efforts to resuscitate them, there was to be no happy ending. The official cause of death was depressurization of the Soyuz cabin. Without the protection of pressure suits, the trio had quickly lost consciousness and expired.[7]

The Soyuz capsule had suffered from an unexpected loss of air pressure, and without pressure suits the cosmonauts were unprotected. Although the Soviets were stunned by this failure, they set to work redesigning the flaw that led to the craft's depressurization, while Salyut 1 continued to orbit the earth unoccupied.

SKYLAB

Those involved in the American space program refused to let the Soviets dominate in any area of space technology, and they set to work on their own space station. Skylab was sent into space on May 14, 1973, and began orbiting 270 miles (434.52km) above the earth. Although the launch of the 75-ton (68 metric ton) station appeared to be flawless, the launch actually damaged shielding and solar panels on the station, which were not discovered until NASA began trying to use various remote-controlled systems used to deploy the solar panels that would provide power to Skylab. On May 25, 1973, after an emergency ten-day training mission, an American crew docked with Skylab and was able to repair the damage. The crew then spent a month in orbit, bringing the station's systems on line and conducting experiments.

Skylab would be occupied several times during its life span, for periods of fifty-nine to eighty-four days, but by 1979 the station had been drifting unoccupied for five years because it could not be boosted into the higher orbit that would make it safe for

INSIDE SKYLAB

Skylab was an economical space station for NASA to build because it was essentially half-finished before its funding was even approved. Skylab was built using the third-stage section of a Saturn rocket, and airtight tanks previously used for fuel were converted into cabins using lightweight flooring and dividers. This kind of equipment recycling made the station easier and less expensive to construct than an entirely new facility.

The main work area inside Skylab was a cylinder 48 feet (14.63m) long and 21 feet (6.4m) in diameter. The partitions were made from a grid with triangular gaps in its mesh, and the crew had special toggles on their boots that could be pushed into these gaps to hold them on the floor and keep them from floating away.

Despite initial problems with a shield that deployed too soon and failed to work, allowing the temperature inside Skylab to rise to 160° F, Skylab spent 170 manned days in space and three missions of astronauts conducted important experiments there.

habitation. Its orbit was degrading quickly, meaning that it was beginning to fall slowly toward Earth. By July 11, 1979, it was completely out of control and entered Earth's atmosphere. Most of it was destroyed upon reentry, although some burning fragments were scattered across hundreds of square miles of Australian outback.

Skylab and the Salyut 1 station shared some of the same technology, but the Soviet Union was several missions ahead in research and design, having attempted two unsuccessful space stations after the Salyut 1 launch. These two parallel space station programs, run by two competing powers, accomplished similar goals, but at a high cost in terms of mistakes, accidents, and deaths. They were also a missed opportunity for scientific cooperation that could have accelerated the world's knowledge of space. Because of the continuing Cold War, such cooperation could not occur as the United States and the Soviet Union vied for political prestige through their accomplishments in space.

MIR

The Soviets had continued to experiment with space stations through many generations of Salyut stations, until the early 1980s when their ongoing research allowed them to construct the first in a new generation of space stations. On February 20, 1986, the Soviet Union launched a new space station named Mir, which means "peace." Mir would be different from its Salyut predecessors because it contained six docking ports. These ports would make it possible for the Soviets to expand the original space station module by adding additional component modules. Mir would become the largest and longest-lived space station in history. Mir also had improved docking methods that would allow transport vehicles to more easily resupply crews, making it possible for astronauts to remain on Mir for longer than ever before. The Soviets also created an unmanned, automated resupply vehicle named Progress which could deliver everything needed by the crew of Mir for both daily life and experiments.

Once Mir's core module was sent into space, the remaining five modules were deployed and locked into place within a four-year period. Once all the modules were successfully locked into place, Mir weighed approximately 150 tons (136 metric tons),

The Soviet Mir was the largest and longest-lived space station in history, continuously occupied from 1986 to 2001.

significantly more than Skylab. Mir would remain in orbit for fifteen years, during which time it was never unoccupied. Several space endurance records were set, including the most days spent on Mir (747 days, for cosmonaut Sergei Avdeyev) and the longest continuous stay (438 days, for cosmonaut Valery Polyakov). Mir finally returned to Earth on March 21, 2001, in a controlled fall that brought it down harmlessly in the Pacific Ocean.

While the Soviets were enjoying their success with Mir, the United States was developing its new space shuttles. These new shuttles would be an alternative to the old Saturn rockets used in the Apollo program which could be used only once and were not cost-effective. The Soviet Union Soyuz rockets were also one-use vehicles. In January 1972, President Richard Nixon had announced the creation of a shuttle program, to build space shuttles that could be launched into space and then land in a manner similar to conventional airplanes. These shuttles would be able to fly over and over, on many missions. However, many people wondered what good this vehicle would be since there was nowhere to fly it to, such as a space station. NASA was hoping that the shuttle program would pave the way for further developments with space station technology, according to Piers Bizony in *Island in the Sky: Building the International Space Station:*

> Everybody at NASA had imagined the shuttle would be just one element of that old dream, an orbiting infrastructure. What was the *point* of a shuttle if it had nowhere to go? Many detailed space station designs had been formulated, but no serious budget requests were put forward. The agency gambled on "proving" their shuttle concept first, and then winning funds for a space station in future years.[8]

NASA also hoped that it could offset some of the costs of the shuttles by making them available to private industry as a cargo vehicle, carrying supplies for private satellites, university experiments, and military purposes. Finally, on April 12, 1981, the first space shuttle, *Columbia*, blasted into orbit. The shuttle program revived public support for the space program, and it also attracted the attention of President Ronald Reagan, who was keenly interested in the shuttle program and the next logical step: the construction of a space station.

STAR WARS

Throughout the Cold War, as the threat of nuclear war between the Soviet Union and the United States had grown, it was inevitable that the idea of a habitat in space should also become a new area for military superiority. Reagan felt strongly that the United States needed to continue strengthening its military defenses, and in an address to the nation on March 23, 1983, he announced a new Strategic Defense Initiative, which came to be

On April 12, 1981, Columbia *became the first space shuttle to be launched into orbit. NASA's successful shuttle program made the idea of a new space station more attractive.*

I SURVIVED SKYLAB

On July 11, 1979, Skylab fell back to Earth after six years in orbit. NASA had originally intended for Skylab to remain in orbit for at least eight years, but because of increasing drag of Earth's atmosphere on the station, slowing its orbitting speed, an early reentry occurred.

For weeks there was mounting speculation all over the world about where the space station would come down, spawning the creation of "Skylab Survival Kits" (hardhats) and "I Survived Skylab" T-shirts. Cash prizes were offered to the first person who could find bits of debris within seventy-two hours of splashdown. The *San Francisco Examiner* offered $10,000 for an authentic piece of Skylab. There were also more serious speculations about the future of space flight if people were likely to be killed by falling debris.

When Skylab fell in the early morning hours of July 12, 1979, it was no longer responding to commands from NASA controllers. Skylab reentered Earth's atmosphere with a series of brightly colored lights and sonic booms, and scattered debris across the southern Indian Ocean and the sparsely populated areas of western Australia.

Stan Thornton of Esperance, a small town in western Australia, collected a small piece of scorched metal from his backyard and flew to San Francisco to collect the $10,000 prize. Australia issued a littering ticket to the United States, but twenty-six years after Skylab's fall, it remains unpaid.

known as Star Wars (a reference to the 1976 George Lucas movie that featured space battles and a warship as big as a planet). Discussing the need for increased defense spending to combat the threat of the Soviet Union's increasing nuclear missile strength, Reagan said:

Let me share with you a vision of the future which offers hope. It is that we embark on a program to counter the awesome Soviet missile threat with measures that are defensive. Let us turn to the very strengths in technology that spawned our great industrial base and that have given us the quality of life we enjoy today. What if free people could live secure in the knowledge that their security did not rest upon the threat of instant U.S. retaliation to deter a Soviet attack, that we could intercept and destroy strategic ballistic missiles before they reached our own soil or that of our allies?[9]

Reagan's Strategic Defense Initiative would include a network of "killer" satellites, laser platforms, and other weapons that would circle the globe and could destroy nuclear missiles before they reached their targets. Many scientists doubted that Star Wars could ever actually become a reality, although it would be a psychological deterrent to the Soviet Union, which could not hope to match the funding the United States would pour into this new defensive plan.

Another aspect of Reagan's plans for a Star Wars defense system was to construct a permanently manned Earth-orbiting space station, which could not only be used for peaceful and scientific purposes, but also as a convenient military outpost in space. In his 1984 State of the Union address, Reagan announced his plans for the space station Freedom, stating that "we can follow our dreams to distant stars, living and working in space for peaceful, economic, and scientific gain."[10] NASA plans called for a 508-square-foot (47.19 sq. m) space station that would accommodate a crew of seven astronauts. It would function as an orbiting repair shop for satellites, a place to assemble spacecraft, an observation point for scientists, and a laboratory. It would also serve defensive purposes, especially if incorporated into the Star Wars plan, as well as a destination for the new space shuttles.

Space station Freedom, however, was never constructed. This was partly the result of an unexpected halt in the space shuttle program. The United States' shuttle development program was grounded in January 1986 after the shuttle *Challenger* exploded shortly after takeoff, killing all the astronauts aboard. Even though the shuttle program resumed thirty-two months later, research and design of the space station had already consumed over $11.4 billion in nine years, without resulting in a single piece of flight-ready equipment. When President Bill Clinton took office in 1993, he demanded a more cost-effective program, which eventually led to the cooperative venture of the International Space Station.

Meanwhile, the Cold War abated with the collapse of the Soviet government in 1991, and the fierce space competition between the United States and Russia (the largest nation of the former Soviet Union) also diminished. Russian president Mikhail Gorbachev and U.S. president George H.W. Bush signed an agreement for cooperation between their two countries' space programs. Bush signed a similar agreement with Gorbachev's successor, Boris Yeltsin, in 1992. As a result of these agreements, a partnership was formed between the Mir space station and the American shuttle program, culminating with a historic docking between Mir and the shuttle *Atlantis* in 1995.

A COOPERATIVE FUTURE

With the lessons learned through the Salyut, Skylab, and Mir space stations, the global scientific community had gained a vast amount of knowledge about building habitats in space. The time had come to apply this technology to a cooperative space station, with many different countries sharing both the benefits and the costs of the projects. This next step in space technology would lead to the construction of the International Space Station.

2

DESIGNING AN INTERNATIONAL SPACE STATION

The years of space rivalry between the United States and the Soviet Union were over, and Reagan's plans for building space station Freedom as part of his Star Wars plan had fallen victim to a new era of economic worries and budget limitations for NASA. A new partnership would have to be formed, a balance of technology and money, to keep the dream of a space station alive.

A HANDSHAKE IN SPACE

On June 29, 1995, for the first time in twenty years, an American spacecraft commander greeted a Russian commander in orbit. Robert Gibson shook hands with Vladimir Dezhurov in a tunnel linking the space shuttle *Atlantis* with the space station Mir. This historic handshake would usher in a new era of cooperative space ventures between the two countries.

This handshake was made possible by a deal signed on September 2, 1993, between U.S. vice president Al Gore and Russian prime minister Viktor Chernomyrdin. This agreement made Russia part of the project to build the space station Freedom, which had been renamed Alpha. In return, the United States would use its space shuttles to help resupply the Russian space station Mir.

The historic agreement was described in an article published by the Facts On File *World News Digest* on September 16, 1993:

> U.S. Vice President Al Gore and Russian Premier Victor S. Chernomyrdin . . . signed an agreement that called for the two countries to jointly design and build an international space station before the end of the decade. The

In 1995 U.S. astronaut Robert Gibson (right) shakes hands with Russian cosmonaut Vladimir Dezhurov in a passageway linking the space shuttle Atlantis *and the space station Mir.*

unprecedented agreement brought to a close decades of Cold War competition in space and drew the focus of developing technology away from the arms race and toward cooperative U.S.-Russian efforts in space exploration. Gore said that with Russian participation, the space station would function years earlier than the U.S. originally had planned, and at a "significantly lower" cost.[11]

Russia would play an important role in the construction of Alpha, which would eventually become the ISS. They would adapt some of their existing space station hardware as building blocks for the new space station. This core would provide temporary propulsion in the form of two main engines which could be used for maneuvering the station in orbit, as well as power so the first component of the ISS could function in space while the rest of the station was assembled around it. America claimed that Russia's involvement in the new space station would speed up the program and save NASA money.

Some skeptics voiced concern at the prospect of allowing Russia to join the American project, especially if Russian aerospace technology began to compete with U.S. companies. Others worried about losing American jobs if much of the space station's construction took place outside of the country. White House science advisor John Gibbons reassured these critics by saying:

> With respect to potential Russian participation . . . no one should confuse the course we are charting as relinquishing control of the space station or exporting jobs out of the US. In developing this cooperative program, we are focusing on areas that will not negatively impact the US aerospace sector. We intend to proceed in a way that protects our vital domestic interests while maximizing the benefit we can derive from fuller interaction with the Russians.[12]

AN INTERNATIONAL PROJECT

Russia, however, would not be the only partner in this new space station project. The European Space Agency would become NASA's other partner in developing the project. The agency, known as ESA, consists of fifteen member countries: Austria, Belgium, Denmark, Finland, France, Germany, Ireland, Italy, the Netherlands, Norway, Portugal, Spain, Sweden, Switzerland, and the United Kingdom. Europe's involvement with American space endeavors was not new. As early as 1969, the United States had approached the European countries about cooperating on a space station. In 1970 Nixon's NASA administrator Tom Paine held preliminary discussions with the three European space organizations that existed at the time. After presenting the United States' space plans, he reported back to the president, "It seems clear that our proposed space station– Space Shuttle systems would obsolete many of their proposed developments before they became fully operational. For this reason, our proposals for international participation are receiving thoughtful attention."[13] Although international cooperation was never achieved on early projects, once NASA began planning the International Space Station with Russia as a partner, the ESA was another natural partner for this huge project. Ultimately Japan, Canada, and Brazil would join the project as well.

Even with a collection of international partners, NASA still needed to secure funding for the space station Alpha. Many U.S. congressmen were uneasy about an alliance with Russia, since that country's shaky economy was a cause for concern. It was feared that Russia would fail to meet its financial obligations to the project, leaving the United States to pick up the entire cost. Russian Space Agency chief Yuri Koptev, while assuring the United States government that Russia was committed to the project, noted that the United States had already gone through nine congressional votes on the fate of the space station, and that Russia did not know the United States would not back out. Adding to the insecurities over funding was the fact that both the ESA and Canada found themselves under budget constraints, cutting the size of their contributions to the station.

Space station opponents introduced a bill in Congress that would have terminated the project, but finally a backup scheme was created for completing the station in the event that Russia reneged on its promises. The termination bill failed and the space station project was saved. Dan Goldin, the head of NASA, praised the House of Representatives for its decision to continue building the station: "It was a vote for America and for the American people, and a vote for our future."[14]

DESIGNING A SPACE STATION

In the months following their agreement to build an international space station, the United States and Russia took several vague proposals from their scientific communities and worked on creating a firm plan for the project. These proposals included using the Mir space station and a second identical Mir component; using the design of the Freedom space station on a smaller scale; using part of either a Russian or U.S. military satellite sys-

A PLEA FOR FUNDING

In July 1995 a plea for continued funding of NASA's programs came from actor Tom Hanks. Hanks had recently starred in the movie *Apollo 13*, which told the story of the April 1970 *Apollo 13* mission, when an onboard explosion nearly doomed the spacecraft to being lost in space. The movie was very popular and reminded the public of NASA's accomplishments in the days of Apollo flights and moon landings.

On July 25, 1995, Hanks visited Capitol Hill and spoke to a group of politicians from both political parties about the importance of continuing space exploration. A few days later, notes Piers Bizony in *Island in the Sky: Building the International Space Station*, he wrote an open letter to Congress:

> I know that such concepts as a permanently manned orbiting science station and other NASA projects are not as glamorous as going to the moon. But to choose not to go into space, to decide that our days of discovery are over . . . would hamper our manifest destiny. I hope you will support full funding for NASA's programs.

The influence of Hanks and the public's increased interest in space travel may have convinced Congress to continue funding NASA and the space station. A congressional motion to cancel the project failed, and in September 1995 Congress passed a bill authorizing a budget of $2.1 billion a year from 1996 to 2002 for the construction of the space station.

tem to construct a station; and building a small station that could be sent into space in a single launch and would require no further construction. The first design for the ISS closely resembled today's station, with two Russian components, the Salyut "space tugboat" and a Mir module, attached to the laboratories of other nations. The ISS would orbit at an altitude of 250 miles (403.34km) above Earth so that it could be reached by the launch vehicles of all the international partners, allowing the best opportunities for a continuous delivery of crews and supplies. This orbit would also provide the best observation point for Earth. The station would be commanded and controlled jointly by the Korolev Control Center near Moscow, Russia, and NASA's Johnson Space Center in Houston, Texas.

Beyond these first two components, the Mir module and the Salyut space tugboat, which were already in existence in Russia, the ISS would require the construction of new elements. The first new component would be built by Russia but financed by NASA. Russia called upon its considerable experience with space stations to make large contributions to the ISS. This first

An artist's concept of the fully completed International Space Station shows all of its modules and solar arrays installed.

contribution was the functional cargo block or control module, and it was later given the name Zarya, which means "sunrise" in Russian. It would contain the control center for the ISS, as well as docking ports, fuel tanks, and solar panels. Zarya would be followed by a second building block for the ISS, a node or linking section named Unity, which would serve as a hub to hold future sections of the ISS.

A system of trusses, or metal grids, would be used to link other sections to these first core modules. Thermal radiators (which disperse excess heat from the electronics on the ISS) and photovoltaic arrays (which convert solar energy into electric power) would be added to create power for the station, as well as more service and docking modules to link shuttles and other spacecraft to the station. The United States and its partner countries would add research and laboratory modules.

Each country expressed its intention to construct various parts of the ISS. Canada would construct a robotic arm that could be used for the assembly and placement of new equipment. Japan expressed interest in constructing a multipurpose research module for space science and technology studies. The ESA agreed to contribute another research module as well as a transfer vehicle to bring supplies to the ISS and boost the station into a higher orbit should its orbit drift closer to Earth, as Skylab's had. Russia's other contributions to the station would include at least two science modules, more solar panels, and an escape vehicle to be used in the event of a disaster on the ISS.

Russia would also provide the reliable Proton rocket to help transport the pieces of the ISS into space. The unmanned Proton rocket was especially good for lifting heavy payloads into space as it was capable of lifting more than twenty tons into orbit. These rockets had flown more than two hundred times since they were introduced in 1965 as a Soviet launcher for military and space purposes, but they were not reusable.

Besides the module Unity, the United States would be responsible for providing a laboratory, eight solar panels, and, most important, the space shuttle, which would transport the building blocks of the ISS into space as well as transporting provisions and astronauts. The reusable shuttles would be well-adapted as a platform for conducting external construction on the ISS, since their cargo bay could be fitted with a robotic arm for lifting and attaching components.

The United States chose a single primary contractor to oversee the building of all of the country's contribution to the ISS. The Boeing Company of Houston, Texas, known for building airplanes, was originally chosen to build an earlier version of the ISS, which would have been a solely U.S. project. Boeing would be responsible for everything from the construction of the large components of the ISS to the communications, tracking, and navigation systems. Boeing would also direct a national industry team made up of major American aerospace companies and

OTHER SPACE STATION DESIGNS

When NASA was considering a design for the space station that would become the ISS, many different ones were presented. These designs had to fulfill all of NASA's requirements for an orbital base, such as being suitable for a wide range of experiments and taking advantage of the characteristics of the space environment such as weightlessness and the lack of atmosphere. Designs were also evaluated on their ability to serve as an intermediate base for exploring the moon and other planets, or possibly for repairing malfunctioning satellites.

The first design was called the "power tower" because of its elongated shape, with eight sets of solar panels at the end of a huge central truss or girder. At the opposite end of the truss would be five modules for the crew, laboratories, and logistics, as well as a docking area for the shuttle.

The second design to be given serious consideration was the "dual-keel" design, in which the huge central truss of the power tower design was replaced by a rectangular truss structure with a horizontal truss aligned through the center. This would distribute the weight of the station more evenly, with four enlarged habitation modules in the center of the structure. Additional modules and experiments could be attached to the outer trusses, away from the central modules.

Ultimately the dual-keel design would be simplified to a single truss to reduce cost and complexity. The design would be further modified to utilize the Zarya module from the Russian Mir program, leading to the ISS design as it exists today.

Russia's powerful Proton rocket blasts into space. The Proton rocket and the U.S. space shuttles share responsibility for lifting pieces of the International Space Station into orbit.

hundreds of smaller contractors, as well as integrating the work of many of the other member countries involved in the ISS.

All the planned ISS components, which would be constructed and deployed over a period of eight years, would be assembled in space, much like a giant puzzle or a building toy of blocks and connecting rods. They would be designed so as to be as simple as possible to put together in space.

THE MODULES

The modules themselves would also utilize the newest technologies in order to make them as safe as possible for the crews who would inhabit the ISS. Each module would have an outer shell of lightweight aluminum, with an additional layer of four-inch (10.14cm)-thick Kevlar (the same material used in bullet-proof vests and automotive tires) as well as a ceramic material. This would create added protection from microscopic bits of grit and tiny meteors that could puncture the space station and cause air leaks.

Each module of the ISS would have a specialized purpose and be dependent on the other modules. This would make it possible to conduct more complex experiments in space, since the area on each specialized module could be devoted to its purpose rather than to the systems required for independent survival. This was a major difference from the Mir space station, where each module could function independently.

The construction of the ISS would not only require the successful completion of the modules and other structures that actually make up the station, but also the organization and creation of a system of launch centers and vehicles to send these components up into space and to provide transportation for crews and supplies.

THE ISS DELIVERY SERVICE

A space station orbiting the earth is much like a deserted island, cut off from the rest of civilization with no source of food or water or even breathable air. In order to survive, its inhabitants must have a supply line to provide them with the necessities for life. The ISS would require an extensive support network of space vehicles and launch sites to keep it supplied with the items necessary for maintenance and existence, and also for its construction.

The cargo fleet of the space world would consist of two different vehicles, the Russian Proton rocket and the U.S. space shuttle. The Proton rocket is an unmanned one-use vehicle that delivers its payload and then plunges back to Earth, burning up upon reentry to the atmosphere. The shuttle, on the other hand, requires human pilots, but can be reused many times as it glides back to Earth and lands much like an airplane.

There are also several other rockets available for transporting payloads to the ISS, including Russia's Soyuz rocket, Europe's Ariane 5 rocket, and Japan's H-IIA rocket. Many of these vehicles were developed for the purpose of boosting satellites into orbit. The Ariane 5 rocket would actually undergo special adaptations making it more suitable for delivering the European Automated Transfer Vehicle (ATV) to a low Earth orbit. This special Ariane rocket, to be called the Ariane 5V (Versatile), is still under development. The Japanese H-IIA rocket is a modified version of the original H-II orbiting plane, an experimental design similar to the space shuttle that suffered two successive launch failures in 1998 and 1999. The H-IIA is capable of carrying large loads and was intended to launch satellites into space for commercial customers. A more powerful, augmented version of the H-IIA will be needed to transport the future Japanese H-II Transfer Vehicle (HTV) into space, where it will function as a cargo ship to carry supplies to the ISS, and then be filled with trash and incinerated upon its return to Earth's atmosphere.

The Russians also have a service vehicle known as the Soyuz TM spacecraft. One of these vehicles is always docked on the ISS as an emergency escape vehicle, although it must be replaced

A Soyuz space capsule (left) and an unmanned Progress vehicle (right) are two Russian-designed space station transport vehicles.

THE BAIKONUR COSMODROME

One of the most interesting results of the new space cooperation between the United States and Russia was access to previously forbidden space technology areas, including the Baikonur Cosmodrome in Kazakhstan. This huge space center, 2,464 square miles (6381.73 sq. km) in area, was once the main Soviet Union launch complex for intercontinental ballistic missiles, which could reach targets on the other side of the world. It was so secret that it was named after a small mining town two hundred miles northeast of its actual location in an attempt to mislead the United States as to its real place and prevent surveillance activity.

Baikonur sits in the middle of an almost uninhabited area, with two separate cultures existing side by side: the technicians and astronauts for the Russian space program, and the camel-riding, wandering nomads who are native to the area. The population of the town of Baikonur once peaked at 120,000 people and has now declined to 30,000. Many of the buildings and facilities of Baikonur have fallen into disrepair, and the site has fallen victim to frequent fires, thefts, and riots.

Baikonur was off-limits to foreigners for many years. Even in the era of cooperation between the Apollo and Soyuz programs, U.S. astronauts were flown in at night, allowed to visit only the launchpad, and then flown out again after dark. This way they could never see the exact extent of the facilities.

Today Baikonur has benefited financially from the new cooperation of the ISS program, as well as other private commercial space ventures that lease space at the site.

every six months because it is only designed to withstand the conditions of space orbit for two hundred days. The Soyuz TM is piloted by astronauts and its descent module returns to Earth using parachutes and a soft-landing engine, while its other two sections separate and burn up in the atmosphere.

Another important part of the ISS fleet is the Russian Progress M spacecraft, which is an unmanned cargo vessel. It can travel to the ISS to deliver supplies and equipment. Once the Progress M has been emptied by the crew of the ISS, it is filled with trash and released to burn up in Earth's atmosphere. The Japanese HTV will be a similar transfer vehicle, and the ESA is also developing its own unmanned transfer vehicle that can automatically deliver cargo to the ISS and then, like the Progress, be released with a cargo of trash.

The ISS presently depends on the Russian Soyuz vessel as a lifeboat for emergency evacuation of the station, but its size limits the crew to three members. NASA and the ESA are developing a crew return vehicle that can return a crew of seven people to Earth at short notice.

The Russians are also developing their own version of the space shuttle, called Kliper. In September 2004 the Russian Space Agency announced that this shuttle would be included in its 2005–15 budget, and that the shuttle's metal hull had already been built. The first launch could take place as early as 2010. The shuttle will ultimately be able to carry six crew members as well as cargo. Kliper will be carried into orbit on a modified Soyuz rocket, and will provide many of the same services to the ISS as the United States' space shuttles.

All of these vehicles, in order to service the ISS in a safe and timely manner, must have facilities on earth for launching and landing.

LAUNCH CENTERS

One of the most famous launch centers in the world is Cape Canaveral in Florida. Originally chosen because of its warm climate and its proximity to the Atlantic Ocean, Cape Canaveral has been used by the United States space program since shortly after World War II. The U.S. space shuttles launch from platforms in the northern part of the Kennedy Space Center complex.

Russia's launch center is located at Baikonur, in the republic of Kazakhstan, which is an arid, desertlike region. This center was constructed in 1955 and contains fourteen launchpads for the heavy Proton rockets, as well as for the Soyuz and Progress spacecraft.

Europe's space launching site is Kourou, located in French Guiana, South America. It is near the equator, so rockets launched from there get a maximum advantage from the west-east rotation of the earth, giving them extra energy. It is primarily

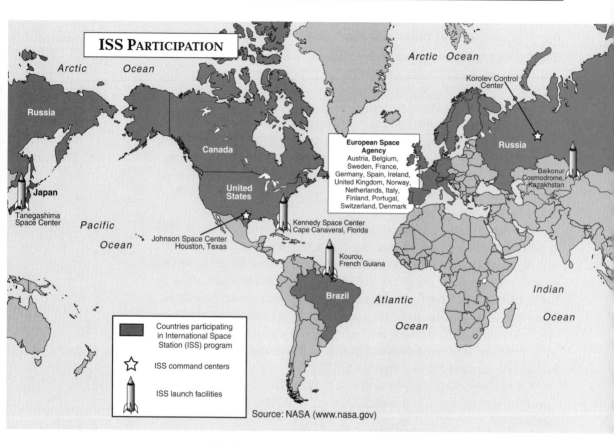

ISS PARTICIPATION

Arctic   Ocean

Arctic Ocean

Korolev Control
Center

Russia

Russia

Canada

European Space
Agency
Austria, Belgium,
Sweden, France,
Germany, Spain, Ireland,
United Kingdom, Norway,
Netherlands, Italy,
Finland, Portugal,
Switzerland, Denmark

Baikonur
Cosmodrome,
Kazakhstan

Japan

United
States

Tanegashima
Space Center

Pacific

Kennedy Space Center
Cape Canaveral, Florida

Ocean

Johnson Space Center
Houston, Texas

Kourou,
French Guiana

Indian

Brazil

Atlantic

Ocean

Ocean

Countries participating
in International Space
Station (ISS) program

ISS command centers

ISS launch facilities

Source: NASA (www.nasa.gov)

responsible for the launch of the Ariane 5 rocket, and will also
be the launch site for the ESA's new ATV, which is being developed as a one-use unmanned cargo vehicle for delivering supplies to the ISS.

Finally, Tanegashima Space Center in Japan is another link
in the chain of launch centers to service the ISS. Located near
the coast of a long, narrow island called Tanegashima, it can
launch spacecraft toward either the east or the south over the
ocean. It contains launch facilities for space vehicles of many
sizes, as well as a tracking station and radar station. New construction facilities and a mobile launch platform have been built
for Japan's experimental vehicles.

This network of launch facilities provides the necessary
highways for the vehicles that will be needed to construct and
maintain the ISS. Located throughout the world, they also back
each other up in the event of an emergency situation or adverse
weather conditions.

With all the space vehicles expected to be flying between the earth and the ISS, it was also necessary to create a new flight control center to oversee this traffic. A new mission control center was built adjacent to the space-shuttle flight control room at the Johnson Space Center. The Russian control room in Korolev also provides flight control to the Russian space vehicles. The flight control technicians at these two control centers monitor the ISS itself and its functions. The ISS requires permanent, twenty-four-hours-a-day monitoring, and to meet this need a new flight control training center was also created. The American and Russian control centers interact with each other in all aspects of ISS operations, and additional flight monitoring is provided by the Japanese and European space centers.

By the end of 1994, the stage had been set for the construction of the International Space Station: Partners had been assembled, a design plan was in place, and the necessary spacecraft and launch centers were ready. It was time to set the first pieces in place.

PREFABRICATING
A SPACE STATION

It would require more than forty assembly missions spread out over eight years to construct the International Space Station. Each component of the ISS would be constructed on the ground, often in many different member countries, and then launched into space for final assembly into the space station itself. These components would have to be constructed according to schedule, delivered to their launch sites, and then sent into space for assembly in the proper sequence.

THE RUSSIAN CORE

The first section of the ISS would be the Russian control module Zarya. This most important core of the space station was built at the Khrunichev Space Research and Production Center near Moscow, although it was largely financed by NASA through a $190-million contract with Boeing. Construction of Zarya began in December 1994, and although the original United States contract financed building only a single module, the Russians used spare parts and their own funds to build a second backup module, in case the first module should be destroyed during a launch failure, or suffer a disastrous systems malfunction. Because Zarya was the central building block for the entire ISS project, a backup module was good insurance against an accident that could put the entire construction project years behind schedule.

Zarya, a 20-ton (18.14 metric ton) cylindrical module, was built according to a design that was originally intended for Russia's Mir space station. More than 42 feet (12.8m) in length and 13 feet (3.96m) in diameter, it had an expected life span in orbit of fifteen years. Zarya would provide two main engines that would allow the station to be maneuvered in orbit, as well as living quarters for ISS astronauts, and was equipped with an 80-foot (24.38m) span of solar panels to generate power, as well as six batteries.

The Zarya control module was scheduled to launch in April 1998, but the Russian Space Agency warned the United States that due to funding problems the control module would not be ready. NASA considered constructing and launching an interim control module to keep the ISS on track, and there was speculation that Russia would be dropped from the ISS program because of its inability to deliver as promised. According to Dan Goldin of NASA, "The fact of the matter is, the Russians have to do what they say they are going to do. We set up a very complex program, and the Russians have not been funding their side."[15]

In 1997 Russian technicians work on the Zarya control module in a research center near Moscow. The module was the first section of the ISS to be launched into space.

The United States and Russia finally agreed that the initial launch would be postponed until mid-1998, and if the Russians did not deliver Zarya in time, then NASA would launch its interim control module instead. President Clinton stated that he was willing to see the United States lend financial help to Russia in order to keep the ISS on track, saying, "If it were required now to help the Russians through this difficult period, which will not last forever, so they could continue to participate, I'd be in favor of it. I think we're doing the right thing with this space station, and we need to stay with it."[16]

Zarya was completed for launch in November 1998, and would soon be followed by the next component of the ISS.

UNITY AND STAR POWER

The second piece of the ISS, the Unity module, was the first U.S.-built section of the space station and was essentially a

A NASA technician inspects a docking port on the Unity module. Other space station modules or spacecraft can attach to Unity at one of its six docking ports.

docking and linking node, or a hub section where additional modules could be attached to the station and space vehicles could dock. It would be attached to the Zarya control module with a preinstalled Pressurized Mating Adapter (a pressurized module to connect the ISS to a docking spacecraft), and would serve as a passageway to living and working areas of the ISS. Unity also contained six docking ports where future modules could be attached. Unity was 18 feet (5.49m) in length and 15 feet (4.57m) in diameter, and was fabricated from aluminum. It also contained a bewildering number of mechanical items—more than fifty thousand—as well as 216 lines for fluids and gases and 121 external and internal electrical cables that carried more than 6 miles (9.66km) of wire, all in a very small space.

Zvezda, or "star" in Russian, was the first contribution to the ISS financed solely by Russia. Zvezda would take over some of the functions that had been temporarily provided by the Zarya module. It would be the central nervous system of the ISS, providing a command and control center, life support systems, permanent living quarters, and the power to boost the ISS's orbit if necessary. Zvezda was similar to the module that created the core of the Mir space station and its hull was originally built in 1985 as a future component of Mir, but it was outfitted with a more modern, German-built computer brain that was paid for by the ESA, and was considered by the United States to be even more advanced than what NASA was using. In addition to its other functions, Zvezda would distribute electrical power to the rest of the ISS and provide data processing and communications, including handling remote commands from ground flight controllers. With four docking ports, it would also be the main docking area for Russian supply vehicles.

Forty-three feet (13.11m) long, with a span of almost 100 feet (30.48m) once its solar arrays were deployed, Zvezda consisted of three pressurized compartments: a small sphere-shaped transfer compartment at the front end, a long cylindrical main work compartment, and another small transfer chamber at the other end. Wrapped around the end of the rear transfer compartment was an unpressurized assembly compartment that would hold external equipment such as propellant tanks, thrusters, and communications antennas. Weighing twenty tons (18,140 kg), Zvezda would be the centerpiece of the ISS.

ZVEZDA SERVICE MODULE

The Zvezda Service Module was launched on July 11, 2000, from the Baikonur Cosmodrome in Kazakhstan. It docked via remote control with the already orbiting Zarya and Unity modules on July 25, 2000. Zvezda is 43 feet (13m) long, weighs 42,000 pounds (15,680kg), and with its solar arrays, has a wingspan of 97.5 feet (29.72m).

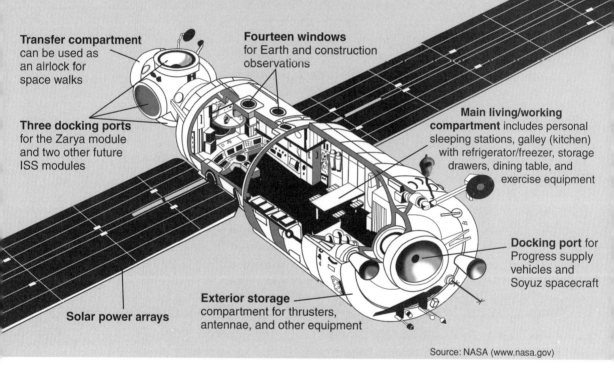

Transfer compartment can be used as an airlock for space walks

Fourteen windows for Earth and construction observations

Three docking ports for the Zarya module and two other future ISS modules

Main living/working compartment includes personal sleeping stations, galley (kitchen) with refrigerator/freezer, storage drawers, dining table, and exercise equipment

Docking port for Progress supply vehicles and Soyuz spacecraft

Solar power arrays

Exterior storage compartment for thrusters, antennae, and other equipment

Source: NASA (www.nasa.gov)

Constructed at the Khrunichev Space Research and Production Center, Zvezda was encased in a protective nose cone, a structure that would prevent damage to the module in transit to the launch site. It was brought to the Baikonur Cosmodrome launching site in Kazakhstan by train.

Zvezda was launched two years behind schedule because of Russia's lack of funding and technical problems. The launch was further delayed by the failure of two Proton launch rockets. The delay of Zvezda's launch brought the ISS project to a standstill. The U.S. Congress was concerned about Russia's ability to fulfill its financial obligations to the project, but the successful completion and launch of Zvezda cemented Russia's part in the space station.

AN ISS BACKBONE

Unlike the previous three modules, the next components of the ISS would provide the first structural backbone for the space station. This exterior framework, a large girder called the Z1 Truss, would house gyroscopes to control the attitude (or tilt) of the ISS, and communications equipment as well as enhanced voice and television capability. The United States' photovoltaic solar arrays would be attached to the truss as a means of generating power. The truss would also provide a place to attach future trusses for the further expansion of the ISS.

Along with the Z1 Truss, another component that would be added to the ISS in the same space flight was a second Pressurized Mating Adapter for future docking of shuttle flights and additional ISS modules. Both of these pieces of equipment were manufactured by the United States.

DESTINY

With the basics of life on the ISS now provided by the first modules put into place, it was time to consider pieces of the ISS that would aid in the station's goals of scientific experimentation and a better understanding of life in space. Realization of these goals would begin with the next module, a laboratory constructed by the United States, named Destiny. According to the space transportation development company Andrews Space and Technology, "The U.S. $1.38 billion Destiny laboratory module [would] enable the International Space Station with the capacity to conduct research 24 hours a day, 365 days a year. This research [was] expected to lay the foundation for a multitude of commercial enterprises in the future."[17]

Destiny was built by Boeing Laboratories, and was 28 feet (8.53m) long and 14 feet (4.27m) in diameter. The lab would be pressurized for human habitation, and consisted of three cylindrical sections and two end cones that would be mated to other station components. Each cone section contained a hatch for the astronauts to use in entering and exiting the laboratory module. Destiny also boasted a window on one side of its center section, made of pure telescope-quality glass and facing Earth.

Destiny was also equipped to hold twenty-four racks of scientific gear or systems equipment. Thirteen of these racks would be dedicated to scientific experiments, while the other eleven racks were used for providing power, cooling water, temperature and humidity control, and air systems. These racks could all be removed or replaced for new experiments or maintenance.

Destiny itself was constructed from aluminum, and the exterior was created in a waffle pattern that added strength to the hull. It was then covered with an insulation blanket to protect it from the extreme temperatures found in space. Destiny also had two shields to protect it from space debris and meteoroids: an intermediate shield made from Kevlar and an aluminum shield that would also reflect the intense sunlight that would otherwise create more work for the ISS air-conditioning system.

Destiny was the first module for the ISS that would focus on experimentation rather than station life support, maintenance, and operations, but it was still just another piece in the puzzle.

ISS MOVING VANS

The next additions to the ISS were not intended to remain in place. Built for the ESA in Italy, they were three MPLMs, or Multi-Purpose Logistics Modules. Named for three important historical Italian artists, Leonardo, Donatello, and Raffaello were unmanned, reusable storage modules meant for bringing new laboratory racks to the science laboratory modules and carrying away old ones. These MPLMs would be placed on board the space shuttle as cargo containers, removed from the shuttle once it had docked with the ISS, and temporarily docked with the Unity node. There, they would have their contents removed and would be refilled with items no longer needed on the ISS before being stowed in the shuttle's cargo bay once again and returned to Earth.

Because the three MPLMs had to function as both station modules and cargo transports, they contained life support, fire detection, electrical distribution, and computer systems. Eventually they would also include refrigerators or freezers for transporting experimentation samples and food to and from the station.

As the components of the ISS were readied, Canada began construction of one of the most complex and vital pieces of the new space station, which would be essential for building and maintaining the new structure in space.

THE AMAZING ARM

The United States' space shuttles were already equipped with a device called the Canadarm, a robotic arm attached near the

The Multi-Purpose Logistic Module Leonardo sits in the space shuttle's open cargo bay, ready for delivery to the ISS.

PIZZA IN SPACE

In July 2000 Russia took advantage of an unusual method of raising money for its financially troubled space program. The Proton launch vehicle that carried the Zvezda module into space displayed a prominent Pizza Hut logo on the side. This display reportedly cost the fast-food pizza chain $1 million, but it was probably one of the most unusual advertising displays ever used. Pizza Hut reportedly also paid an enormous sum to the Russian Space Agency in exchange for filming the first space pizza delivery, although Pizza Hut officials decided not to make this footage into a television commercial.

The Russian Space Agency created a company called the Space Marketing Center to handle commercial activities, including the international marketing of space products and space services. Other promotional activities on the ISS have included promotional videos for Radio Shack, Lego, and *Popular Mechanics*. Russian astronauts actually conducted an experiment with Lego toys and photographed a Lego banner and three hundred Lego "alien" figures that were then given away as prizes in a contest.

It is expected that space promotion, funding from private commercial enterprises, and ultimately tourism will provide alternative methods of financial support for increasingly expensive space programs.

cargo bay of the shuttle that was used for lifting equipment or capturing objects in space, such as satellites in need of repair. The ISS, however, would be equipped with an even bigger and better version of this arm, the amazing Canadarm 2. This arm would be essential in the ISS construction:

Building a brand new space station is a big job. Just ask the assembly crews of the International Space Station (ISS). They have to attach modules weighing tons, extend solar panels longer than a bus, and haul equipment to and from the space shuttle. It sounds like these hardworking astronauts [will need] a hand. . . . Now, thanks to the Canadian Space Agency (CSA), they're going to get one. . . . "Canadarm 2 is a bigger, smarter, and more grown-up version of the shuttle's robotic arm," said Chris Lorenz, CSA's manager of mission operations. "It's part of Canada's investment in the space station program."[18]

Canadarm 2 weighed in at over 3,600 pounds (1,633kg) and would be more than 57 feet long (17.37m) when fully extended. It would be capable of handling large payloads of equipment as well as helping to dock the space shuttles, but the most amazing thing about it was the way in which it moved. Unlike the original Canadarm, which was attached to a mounting just outside a shuttle's payload or cargo bay, the Canadarm 2 would not be tied down to one spot on the ISS. Instead, it had a "hand" on each end, which could grasp special anchors called grapple fixtures located on different parts of the space station. By flipping end over end between these anchor points, the Canadarm 2 could move like an inchworm all over the ISS. This would give it a much wider range of mobility and usefulness. The arm also had seven motorized joints, making it more agile than a human arm, and it was much more maneuverable than the smaller fixed Canadarm.

The Canadarm 2 would first be controlled by two robotic workstation consoles inside the Destiny laboratory module, but eventually it would be controlled from a module due to be launched in the future: the Cupola, a windowed module that could provide astronauts with an even better view of the entire ISS, the robotic arm, and docking shuttles. The Cupola module was completed by the ESA in August 2004, but is not expected to be launched to the ISS until 2009.

The Canadian Space Agency also built a ground control center just for the Canadarm 2 at its Saint-Hubert, Quebec, headquarters, linked directly to NASA's mission control in Houston, Texas. While the ISS crewmembers would actually control the arm, the personnel on the ground would provide support and troubleshooting.

Canadarm 2 was intended to be only the first piece of the space station's Mobile Servicing System. This system would also include a Canadian-built Mobile Base System (MBS), a small truck that could move along rails on the outside of the ISS. The Canadarm 2 would be able to ride this MBS to various parts of the space station, which would be faster than inch-worming end

ISS ROBOTIC ARM

This three-part system is a key element in the International Space Station's assembly and maintenance.

Special Purpose Dexterous Manipulator

Also known as the Canada Hand, this is a smaller two-armed robot that can perform more delicate tasks than Canadarm2. About 11.5 feet (3.5m) long, each arm has seven joints plus sensors, lights, and video equipment. Installation scheduled for 2007.

Canadarm2

Moving end over end like an inchworm, Canadarm2 is 57.7 feet (17.6m) long and has seven joints with full rotation. The arm has four color cameras: one at each end of the arm, and two at the elbow. Each end of the arm can latch onto various station locations to anchor itself and move forward. Installed April 2001.

Mobile Base System

A work platform and storage area for the arm which moves along rails covering the length of the space station's main trusses. Added June 2002.

Source: Canadian Space Agency (www.space.gc.ca)

over end. The other piece of the servicing system would be a special "Canada Hand" for one end of the Canadarm 2. This hand would also be a complex robot with two arms and a sophisticated system that would allow it to touch and feel much like a human hand. Equipped with lights, a video camera, and tool holders, the hand could perform more sophisticated operations such as installing batteries and computers. This would reduce the time that astronauts had to spend in the dangerous environment of space.

To some people the Canadarm 2 and its components seemed more like a construction toy than a space tool. According to NASA, "An inchworming space arm equipped with a robotic super-Hand? It sounds like a wonderful Lego kit! Indeed, Canadarm 2 consists of many Lego-like 'on-orbit replaceable units' (ORU's). 'You can basically take the arm apart in Lego fashion and replace units as needed,' added Ken Podwalski, a Canadian Space Agency scientist."[19]

The Canadarm 2 would be almost the last component of this stage of the ISS assembly. The final piece of this phase would be an airlock called Quest.

QUEST

The Quest airlock was necessary to the ISS because it would provide a universal way to exit the ISS for space walks. An airlock was an airtight chamber, located between two areas of unequal pressure, such as the ISS and space itself. The airlock allowed the air pressure to be regulated in order to help astronauts move between these two areas. According to the Web site SpaceRef.com:

> The Joint Airlock (also known as "Quest") is provided by the U.S. and provides the capability for ISS-based Extravehicular Activity (EVA) using either a U.S. Extravehicular Mobility Unit (EMU) or Russian Orlon EVA suits. Before the [Quest] airlock, EVA's were performed from either the U.S. Space Shuttle (while docked) or from the Transfer Chamber on the Service Module. Due to a variety of system and design differences, only U.S. space suits could be used from the Shuttle and only Russian suits could be used from the Service Module. The Joint Airlock alleviates this short term problem by allowing either (or both) space suit systems to be used.[20]

The Quest airlock consisted of two compartments: a crew airlock where astronauts and cosmonauts could exit the ISS, and an equipment airlock designed for storing gear. This second compartment could also be used for overnight "campouts," in which nitrogen is purged from astronauts' bodies before they go

THE SUPER GUPPY

NASA has long used cargo planes for transporting spacecraft components from the manufacturing site to the launch site, including equipment for the Gemini, Apollo, and Skylab programs. These aircraft are called guppies and were first designed as cargo planes in 1962 by Aero Spacelines of California. Guppies were designed to carry larger and heavier loads than normal cargo vehicles, requiring them to be bigger and more powerful than regular cargo airplanes.

NASA is currently using an aircraft called the Super Guppy to transport ISS components. The present Super Guppy plane was acquired from the European Space Agency (ESA) as part of an ISS barter agreement. NASA transported the ESA's experiment equipment to the ISS on two shuttle flights, and the ESA provided the Super Guppy in exchange.

The Super Guppy can also be leased from NASA by the United States government when needed, and the fees for leasing contribute to the operating expenses of the plane.

The Super Guppy has a cargo compartment that is 25 feet (7.62m) tall, 25 feet wide, and 111 feet (33.83m) long. It can carry more than 26 tons (23.59 metric tons) of cargo. This plane has a unique hinged nose that can open more than 200 degrees, allowing large pieces of equipment (such as ISS components) to be loaded and unloaded from the

front. The Super Guppy has also been outfitted with a special cradle to be used when carrying ISS segments.

NASA workers unload an ISS component from the Super Guppy. The Super Guppy can hold much larger pieces of cargo than a regular plane.

The Quest airlock is maneuvered into position by the space station's robotic arm. Astronauts use the airlock to enter and exit the ISS during space walks.

on space walks the following day. This prevents a condition known as the bends, or decompression sickness, where nitrogen bubbles form in the blood.

The Quest was equipped with lighting, external handrails, and supply lines for water, wastewater, and oxygen. It also provided communications gear and the support systems needed for the use of the space suits that would be worn on space walks outside of the ISS. Stations inside the airlock would assist the astronauts in getting into and out of their space suits. It also contained racks for batteries, power tools, and other supplies in its equipment storage area.

THE NEXT STAGE

The next phase of the ISS construction would begin with the Russian-made Pirs docking module. Designed and built by the Russians at the Korolev Control Center near Moscow, Pirs was slightly egg-shaped, almost 14 feet (4.27m) long and over 8 feet (2.44m) in diameter. Pirs, which is the Russian word for "pier", would provide additional docking space for Russian spacecraft. This was especially important because Pirs would provide extra

IMAX

A successful method used for publicizing the ISS has involved the use of IMAX filmmaking. IMAX filmmaking results in a movie that is played in a special theater, with images up to eight stories high and wrap-around sound that gives the audience a three-dimensional experience. The IMAX Corporation used twenty-five astronauts and cosmonauts to shoot more than 12 miles (19.31km) of film in space between December 1998 and July 2001. This film was used to create a documentary called *Space Station 3D*, released in 2002.

Space Station 3D, which chronicles the construction of the ISS in a 3-D format, is the first movie actually shot in space. The flight crews who did the IMAX filming were given special training on the equipment and filming techniques. In order to make a 3-D movie that is convincing to the audience, it is necessary to keep the camera moving as much as possible. The astronauts filming outside the ISS accomplished this through several techniques, including one called "human dollying" where one astronaut held the camera and another pushed or pulled him to create movement.

Producer Toni Myers talks about her orbiting film crew on the IMAX Space Station Web site:

> The crews actually worked very, very hard when they were filming on-orbit for us. We had to accomplish 90 percent of our filming in the few days when the shuttle was docked to the Station. And that, of course, was the peak busiest time for both the visiting shuttle crew and the resident crew. It's miraculous that they got the scenes that they did. Talk about the pressures of filmmaking!

An ISS astronaut lugs bulky IMAX camera equipment through the Zvezda service module.

clearance for ships docking underneath the Zvezda module. Before Pirs existed Progress spacecraft had to be undocked in order to allow an arriving Soyuz craft to dock. Pirs would also give the astronauts an additional exit and entrance for Russian-based space walks outside of the ISS.

After the construction of the Pirs module, the only remaining U.S.-built pieces of the ISS were a truss system called the Integrated Truss Structure, a ten-truss system of girders that would support more radiator assemblies for disposing of excess heat, as well as power distribution modules, a UHF (ultrahigh-frequency) antenna, and the rails for Canada's Mobile Servicing System truck. Once the trusses were assembled in space, they would complete a 365-foot (111.25m) long span across the ISS.

According to ISS program manager Bill Gerstenmaier, the construction of the trusses signified that the end of the ISS component construction was drawing near:

> The shipment [to NASA] of this [final truss] segment signals that the fabrication of all U.S.-built International Space Station core components has been completed. But the most complex and challenging work is ahead as we continue to assemble the truss segments in orbit, multiplying and expanding the Station's power system. When this final truss segment is attached . . . we will be in the home stretch of Station assembly.[21]

Once these final pieces were completed, the trusses were ready for launch and assembly in orbit. The greatest challenge in the construction of the ISS, however, had been taking place since 1998, as all these various components were carried as payload aboard various launch vehicles and brought to their construction site in space for assembly. By the time the truss segments were built, there were already more than 390,000 pounds (176,901kg) of station components in orbit and approximately 110,000 additional pounds (49,895kg) on the ground ready for launch. But the actual pieces of the ISS were only half the story: Putting them together more than 200 miles (322km) above the earth would be even more challenging.

A Construction Site in Space

The actual assembly of the ISS components took place in the same sequence as their construction, meaning that as soon as a module was built, it was launched into space and attached to the space station, rather than stockpiling the different modules and assembling them all at once. This enabled the astronauts to begin living and working on the ISS as soon as the first life support modules were in place.

Before they could start assembling the ISS, the astronauts would need to live and work on a space station. It was in this respect that the new partnership between the Russians and the United States first became valuable.

THE SHUTTLE-MIR PARTNERSHIP

One aspect of the 1993 agreement between Gore and Chernomyrdin was that the United States' space shuttles would begin rendezvousing and docking with the Russian space station Mir, meaning that they would travel into space to the location of Mir and then dock with the station, enabling the U.S. astronauts to go aboard. This would prepare both countries for the joint effort of building and maintaining a cooperative space station. From February 1994 through June 1998, the shuttles *Atlantis* and *Discovery* flew eighteen missions either orbiting or docking with the Mir station. These flights provided the astronauts with valuable experience in space travel aboard the shuttle and life on a space station.

The shuttle-Mir cooperation required astronauts from these two formerly competing countries to learn to adjust to each other's methods and training techniques. Norman Thagard, a U.S. astronaut who had already flown four flights on the shuttle, was the first American to experience this new collaboration, and it was not always a smooth operation, according to Peter Bond:

Having experienced at first hand the difficulties in becoming proficient in an unfamiliar language, the very different training techniques used at Star City [a Russian space training facility] near Moscow, the idiosyncrasies of Russian technology and attitude to authority, Thagard found his task to be harder than anticipated. "The cultural isolation is extreme," Thagard confided. "For an American on board a Russian space station, you're the only English speaker on board in general. There were times when I went 72 hours without speaking to an English-speaking person." The lack of communication with colleagues and the outside world, particularly his family, took its toll. "All of those things start to weigh heavily after a while," he said. "If I had been looking at six months [on the Mir] I would have been real worried that I wasn't going to make it."[22]

This cooperation was very valuable, despite the difficulties involved, because it gave the American astronauts firsthand

A Russian cosmonaut (left) and an American astronaut anchor themselves to the floor while working in the ISS's Destiny lab in 2004.

training and experience in the Russian space station and its systems, as well as docking the shuttle with Mir. They also benefited from the Russians' experiences with space stations and the Russians benefited from the availability of the shuttles to help bring supplies and crews to the Mir station.

By the end of the shuttle-Mir cooperation in 1998, the Russians and Americans had gained valuable technical expertise to

Astronauts install the ISS's truss section as they float hundreds of miles above Earth. Astronauts undergo extensive training to learn how to assemble ISS components in the weightlessness of space.

aid them in the tremendous project of building the ISS and had learned how to work together and solve problems as a team. According to NASA's ISS program manager, Randy Brinkley:

> We tend to learn more from our difficulties and our failures and our problems than we do from our successes, and whereas people may look critically at some of the problems on Mir . . . those things have had a tremendous benefit for us in terms of understanding not only the causes, but also the corrective action and ensuring that we're able to apply those to the International Space Station. . . . Having worked through those difficulties together has created a significant bond between the American and Russian team . . . and that relationship and confidence in one another, understanding, and trust have . . . flowed over into the International Space Station.[23]

With the completion of the shuttle-Mir training missions, the stage was now set for launching the first components of the ISS and getting started on the creation of a construction site in space.

PREPARATIONS FOR BUILDING IN ORBIT

The ISS was an enormous project in that it would not be launched from Earth as a completed unit. Each of the components that had been built on the ground by various international ISS participants would need to be launched into space and then assembled there, high above the earth's surface and in the difficult and dangerous conditions of space.

This kind of project would combine the usual problems of any construction site with the added difficulties of ensuring life support systems for the astronauts and coping with weightlessness in space. NASA describes this process on its Web site:

> With precise grace, an overhead crane swings a 10-ton building block into position. Then, workers move in, climbing on to the structure and using hand and power tools to bolt the pieces together. It is a workaday scene that could be found on almost any city street corner, but this construction site is 250 miles up in the airless

reaches of space, where conditions alternate hourly between freezing and searing. The construction workers are astronauts, the cranes are a new generation of space robotics and the skyscraper taking shape is the International Space Station.[24]

NASA knew that it would need to be prepared to deal with these unusual construction conditions, both in terms of equipment and training of astronauts. These preparations began more than ten years before the first ISS component was launched into orbit. The time spent on the Mir space station was one part of this training program. Astronauts also trained by practicing the assembly of ISS components while submerged in huge pools of water that simulated weightlessness, a sort of dress rehearsal for space walking. New space suits with easily replaceable parts were developed that were easier to adjust, instead of requiring specialized and time-consuming adjustments on Earth. These suits also had new gloves with improved dexterity, special heaters for the astronauts' fingertips, new radios that allowed up to five people to talk at once, and emergency jet packs that would allow astronauts to fly back to the ISS if they became untethered while working. These modifications, in addition to the new robotics such as the Canadarm 2, would help make the in-orbit assembly of the ISS easier and safer.

The ISS was ultimately planned to weigh a million pounds (453,592 kg) and would require the assembly of more than one hundred different components launched on forty-six different space flights, and each component would have to be bolted, latched, wired, plumbed, and fastened together. Such an endeavor would be difficult to accomplish on the ground; up in space, where even the smallest tasks are difficult, it would require extraordinary skill. Despite these obstacles, NASA and the other ISS countries prepared to launch Zarya, the first ISS module, in November 1998.

THE FIRST MODULE

The ISS modules would be launched through a series of missions interspersed with other space flights that would deliver materials, supplies, and fresh crews to the ISS. The first mission would deliver into orbit the first piece of the giant ISS puzzle. Zarya, the Russian-built but U.S.-funded control module, was

WORK CLOTHES IN SPACE

Helmet assembly with lamps, camera, and gold sun filter in visor

Life support backpack system (oxygen, batteries, fans, radio)

Hard upper torso with fiberglass shell under fabric

Attached booklet with checklist of construction and maintenance tasks

Gloves with heaters and loops to hold tools

Underneath it all, a liquid cooling and ventilation garment (like long underwear)

Maximum absorption garment for urine collection

Suit fabric has fourteen layers to protect astronauts from heat, cold, and micrometeors

Lower torso assembly includes pants, built-in boots, and rings for attaching safety tethers

Source: NASA (www.nasa.gov)

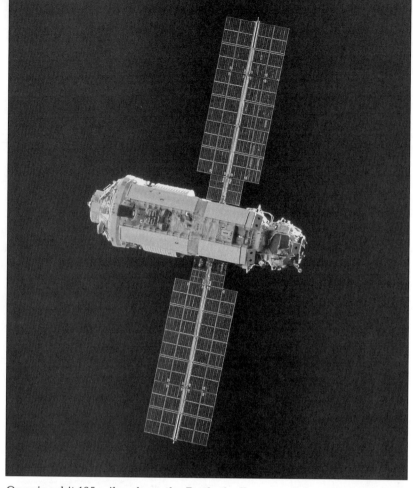

Once in orbit 125 miles above the Earth, the Zarya module unfolded its solar panels and waited to be joined with the Unity module, the second piece of the ISS.

brought to its launch site at the Baikonur Cosmodrome in January 1998 to begin launch preparations, even though it would not actually be sent into space for ten months. The module was loaded with equipment, pressure tested, and fueled. It was then fitted with a protective shroud or covering to protect its mating adapter (where future segments of the ISS would be attached) during its ascent through Earth's atmosphere.

Zarya was then attached to the Proton launch vehicle, the rocket that would carry it into space, and taken by train to the launchpad, where it was lifted into a vertical position. The final connections were made between Zarya and its rocket, and fuel was added to Zarya's tanks. Three days later, a commission representing all of the member countries of the ISS met and confirmed that they were prepared to proceed. It was time to send Zarya into space and begin the ISS construction project.

As the Proton rocket left the launchpad and started on its path into space, where Zarya would orbit 125 miles (201.17km) above Earth, it was hailed as the first step in a long process, according to a CNN report:

> "This is a historic day for it sets the foundation for the new station," said Russian Defense Minister Igor Sergeyev. "It is important not only scientifically but also politically because it was established on the basis of international cooperation," he told Reuters [news service]. Space officials from 16 nations taking part in the project cheered as the rocket soared into the cloudy sky above the central Asian steppe from the Baikonur launch pad.[25]

Once in orbit, Zarya's protective shroud split in half and was discarded. Zarya then went through a series of preprogrammed commands that automatically activated its systems and deployed its solar power arrays and communications antennas. The module was now ready for the addition of the next piece of the ISS, the Unity module, which would take place only a few weeks later.

Joining the First Pieces

The Unity module would be carried into space by the United States' space shuttle *Endeavour*. Unity had been brought to Kennedy Space Center on June 23, 1998, for final preparations and testing. It went through many final pressurization and leakage tests before it was purged with clean, dry air for its trip into space. On November 13, 1998, Unity was placed inside the payload bay on the shuttle *Endeavour*.

On December 4, 1998, *Endeavour* lifted off from Kennedy Space Center and climbed into space. The next day, the crew of *Endeavour* was awakened by a call from Chris Hadfield at Mission Control in Houston: "It's time to get ready to build the International Space Station."[26]

After a day spent on final inspections of the Unity and the equipment that would be used to attach it to Zarya, the crew of *Endeavour* was finally ready to perform the procedure. Using the shuttle's Remote Manipulator System (RMS), Unity was slowly lifted from its storage position inside the shuttle bay. It had to be moved slowly because there was less than an inch

(2.54cm) of clearance on either side between Unity and the walls of the payload bay. Astronaut Nancy Currie used the RMS to turn Unity to a vertical position and then its engine thrusters were fired, moving it into position to mate it to an Orbiter Docking System on *Endeavour*. Docking Unity with *Endeavour* allowed the astronauts to enter Unity without performing a space walk and complete the necessary preparations for Unity's docking with Zarya.

On day four of the shuttle mission, Currie used *Endeavour's* RMS to grab Zarya, which had been orbiting at a slightly higher altitude than the shuttle. After successfully capturing the module, Currie started to maneuver the biggest piece of equipment that the shuttle's RMS had ever manipulated. Positioning Zarya so that it was just a few inches above the Unity's docking ring, Currie fired the shuttle's thrusters and Zarya and Unity were joined, still attached to the shuttle cargo bay and its Orbiter

The space shuttle's robotic arm holds Zarya in place while the Unity module sits upright in the shuttle's cargo bay, ready for docking.

Astronauts use power wrenches to connect the Zarya and Unity modules. After thirteen days of work in December 1998, the two ISS modules were joined permanently.

Docking System. Linked together, Zarya and Unity projected 75 feet (22.86m) above the shuttle. Now the astronauts could perform the necessary space walks to join cables and other attachments between the two modules of the ISS.

It took thirteen days for the astronauts to complete all the necessary work to connect Unity and Zarya permanently. Accessing Unity from the shuttle's Orbiter Docking System, two astronauts (one Russian and one American) floated side by side into the ISS. They were able, on December 10, 1998, to open the hatch from Unity to Zarya and enter that module. The first two portions of the ISS had been joined.

On December 15, 1998, the shuttle *Endeavour* undocked from the new ISS and did a fly-around to inspect the infant space station. *Endeavour* returned to Earth and touched down at the Kennedy Space Center, where crowds of people on the runway greeted the crew. The first ISS assembly mission was over, but the construction had barely begun.

BUILDING BLOCKS

After the successful joining of Zarya and Unity, the ISS was dormant for six months before the space shuttle *Discovery* and another crew visited the station to leave supplies and equipment for the next construction mission. This equipment included two cranes that would be attached to the exterior of the ISS and used for future construction procedures. But due to delays in Russia's delivery of the Zvezda module, it was eleven months before another astronaut would step inside the ISS.

On July 12, 2000, a Russian Proton rocket carrying the Zvezda module was launched from the Baikonur Cosmodrome, twenty-six months behind the original ISS schedule. Once it was placed in its orbit, Zvezda successfully deployed all its solar panels, antennae, and other external fittings. The addition of Zvezda to the ISS, however, would be different from the hands-on joining of Unity and Zarya; it would be completely automated and performed by Russian ground control. If the automatic docking did not work, two Russian cosmonauts who had been trained to complete the docking manually would be launched aboard a Soyuz spacecraft.

Many ISS officials worried about the docking, according to space policy analyst David Webb:

> This particular part of the station is fundamental to the whole construction project—and it's also the one single, potential point of failure. So this mission, in a sense, is like crossing a huge river. If we make it, we're pretty much home free. But if we don't, I see a lot of trouble for the entire space program.[27]

Fortunately, the automatic docking system worked as planned. Two weeks after liftoff, on July 26, 2000, Zvezda pulled in at the rear docking port on Zarya. The station now had its main control center and living quarters. The third piece of the ISS was now in place.

ADDING A BACKBONE

In October 2000, after several other missions delivered additional supplies to the ISS and made further progress with setting up the station, the shuttle *Discovery* lifted off from Kennedy Space Center with a crew of seven, a Pressurized Mating Adapter, and the Z1 Truss that would become the backbone of the ISS. According to space shuttle program manager Ron Dittemore:

> The foundation for the International Space Station has been laid and this mission begins the true station build-up in orbit. With multiple space walks planned, and multiple components to attach, we're taking the level of complexity up a notch over the past few station construction flights.[28]

Discovery docked with the ISS on October 13, 2000, and the next day the Z1 Truss was unloaded from the shuttle's cargo bay

9/11 FROM SPACE

On September 11, 2001, terrorists hijacked four airplanes, crashing two of them into the World Trade Center towers in New York City. The crew of the ISS was in the middle of a radio conference with a flight surgeon when he told them that they were having a "very bad day on the ground" and then gave them as much information about the terrorist attacks as he could. Checking a map on their computer, they discovered that they would soon be passing over New York City. They crowded around the ISS to find the window with the best view of the city, and started filming. They were able to capture video footage of the plumes of smoke rising from the ruins of the two towers. The next day NASA broadcast these images on television. Astronaut Frank L. Culbertson describes what he saw in Peter Bond's book, *The Continuing Story of the International Space Station*:

> There was a large plume of smoke coming from Lower Manhattan and streaming off to the south. We were too far away to see much in the way of detail, but we could see where in the city it was, and there was also a shroud of smoke over the large part of the city. It was quite a disturbing sight . . . and very heartbreaking.

using *Discovery*'s robotic arm, and put into place on Unity's exterior. The new Pressurized Mating Adapter, which would allow components to be joined and maintain a pressurized atmosphere between them, was put into place on the other side of Unity and latched. Astronauts also completed additional preparations for the Destiny laboratory module, which would be installed during a later mission, as well as installing equipment on the new truss, including power units, cables, and antennas. Now the stage was set for the first resident crew that would actually occupy the ISS.

THE FIRST RESIDENTS

On October 31, 2000, seventeen years after Reagan first proposed the construction of a space station, a Soyuz rocket blasted off from the Baikonur Cosmodrome carrying the first astronauts to actually live on the ISS. NASA flight director John Curry commented: "I'd say there's a decent chance that [today] may in fact be the last day that we don't have humans in space."[29] One of the tasks that the crew performed after settling in to the station was to install a new solar array on the Z1 Truss to provide even more power for the station.

On the crew's one hundredth day in space, the shuttle *Atlantis* docked at the ISS to deliver the next piece of the station: the Destiny science laboratory. Destiny would have to be removed from *Atlantis*'s cargo bay and put into place, and this was accomplished with what NASA called "a dazzling display of robotics finesse and space walking skill,"[30] as quoted in Peter Bond's book, *The Continuing Story of the International Space Station*. Using the shuttle's robotic arm, the ISS crew removed a Pressurized Mating Adapter from the end of the Unity module and placed it temporarily on the station's truss. Then they removed Destiny from the shuttle bay, swiveled it 180 degrees, and moved it into position on Unity, in the place where the mating adapter had been previously.

On a second space walk the next day, the crew removed the Pressurized Mating Adapter from its temporary position on the truss and placed it on the end of the Destiny module, where it would become the docking port for all future space shuttle flights. They also attached a base to the exterior of Destiny to be used for the ISS's future robotic arm.

On March 8, 2001, another *Discovery* shuttle flight brought a replacement crew and the MPLM Leonardo, the first of the

On November 2, 2000, Russia's Mission Control Center watches as the first three International Space Station residents celebrate their arrival on the station.

reusable storage units built in Italy for the space station. During a space walk, Leonardo was maneuvered into place on the Unity module and the crew started unloading more than five tons of supplies for the ISS. Leonardo would be filled with waste, outdated hardware, and luggage to be returned to Earth. Leonardo was then unberthed from Unity, placed back inside *Discovery*'s cargo bay, and latched into place in a special cradle. When the shuttle left the ISS, it also carried the station's first resident crew home after 136 days in space. During this time, the ISS had hosted three separate shuttle flights and had more than doubled in size and power.

A ROBOTIC HANDSHAKE

The rapid pace of construction on the ISS continued with another shuttle flight on April 19, 2001. The shuttle *Endeavour* lifted off from Florida carrying a Spacelab pallet loaded with the Canadarm 2 and a UHF antenna.

The pilot used the shuttle's robotic arm to lift the pallet out of *Endeavour*'s cargo bay and place it in a special cradle outside the Destiny module. Then two other shuttle astronauts floated into the shuttle's payload bay and deployed the new antenna.

A WALK IN SPACE

In order to construct the ISS, astronauts had to perform many hours of space walks. While it is necessary in terms of both productivity and safety for these astronauts to focus on the job at hand, a space walk outside the ISS is also an unforgettable event, according to Jim Reilly, an astronaut who performed a series of space walks in July 2001. He recounts a piece of advice he received from astronaut Yuri Usachev in Peter Bond's book, *The Continuing Story of the International Space Station*:

"When you're working, just make sure you take a couple of seconds to just look up every once in a while, and look around." That was the best piece of advice he gave me, because every once in a while, just for 10 seconds, I'd stop and look around, and see what part of the planet I was over, and look at the horizon. . . . One time when I had a chance to hang out on the bottom of the station, the sunset was coming. I left my lights off so I could watch the Sun go down. And as it went down, the stars started popping out. Of course they don't twinkle. They're all different sizes, and even different colors, in space. . . . At night you can see lightning flashes from thunderstorms on the surface down below. And as I was watching all this, we flew through the edges of the aurora, kind of green and white curtains as we flew past. It was pretty spectacular.

On the following day, the two crews of the shuttle and the ISS met for the first time and spent ten hours working with the two robotic arms: the Canadarm 2 and the shuttle's own robotic arm. From a workstation inside the Destiny module, ISS crew member Susan Helms commanded the new Canadarm 2 to "walk" off its pallet. The free end of the arm grasped a grapple fixture on the exterior of Destiny, ready to do its first lifting job the next day. Then the shuttle's robotic arm began unloading the cargo module Raffaello and carried it to its berth on Destiny.

Later the ISS crew opened a panel on the exterior of Destiny and connected power, computer, and video cables to the

Canadarm 2. The arm could then be disconnected from its pallet and controlled from inside Destiny. Eventually the Canadarm 2 would be used to return its travel pallet to the *Endeavour* in a historic robotic handshake, as the Canadarm 2 lifted the pallet and handed it over to the shuttle's robotic arm.

During testing of the Canadarm 2, it was discovered that the arm had a faulty computer chip that blocked some of the control commands from reaching the arm's elbow and wrist joints. It was critical to get the arm working correctly, since it would be essential to the installation of the next piece of the ISS, the Quest airlock. The Canadian Space Agency and NASA transmitted a software patch from Earth to repair the arm.

Canadarm 2's first real test came with the launch of the shuttle *Atlantis* in July 2001, with the Quest airlock in its cargo bay. After docking with the ISS, the astronauts removed heating cables, which had protected it from the cold of space, from the Quest. Using the Canadarm 2, the ISS crew grappled the mushroom-shaped airlock, lifting it out of the shuttle bay and moving it to its berth on the right side of the Unity module. Astronauts then attached heating cables to the airlock, as well as foot restraints that would help them during their next space walk.

The successful installation of the Quest airlock was celebrated with a ribbon-cutting ceremony inside it. With the addition of this module, the volume of the ISS had now increased to approximately 15,000 cubic feet (424.75 cubic meters), larger than a three-bedroom house. It also marked the end of phase 2 of the ISS construction.

THE NEXT PHASE

In September 2001, the next element of the ISS and the beginning of the next phase of its construction was launched aboard an unmanned Russian Soyuz rocket. The Pirs module, which would be used as an airlock (an area where astronauts could move from the pressurized ISS to the unpressurized environment of space) and a docking port, was connected to the docking port on the Zvezda module by an automatic docking system. The rocket and the new module approached the ISS from below and behind, and then the ISS's own thrusters moved it into the proper orientation for docking. The crew made sure that there was a good seal between the new module and the Zvezda module, and then they started equalizing the pressure between the

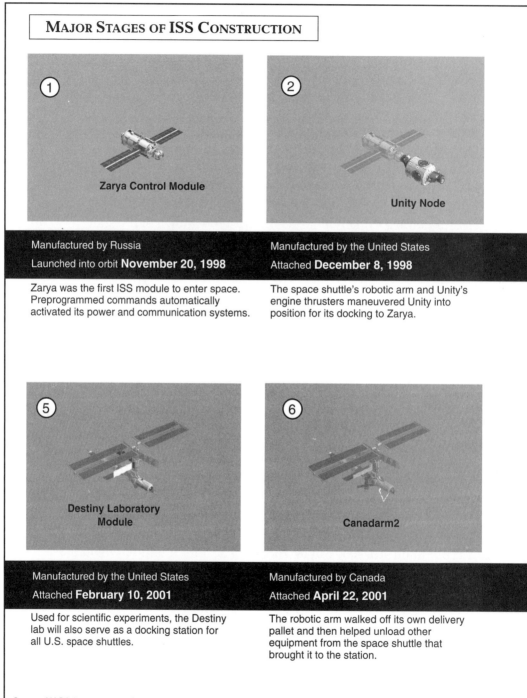

MAJOR STAGES OF ISS CONSTRUCTION

①

Zarya Control Module

②

Unity Node

Manufactured by Russia

Launched into orbit **November 20, 1998**

Zarya was the first ISS module to enter space. Preprogrammed commands automatically activated its power and communication systems.

Manufactured by the United States

Attached **December 8, 1998**

The space shuttle's robotic arm and Unity's engine thrusters maneuvered Unity into position for its docking to Zarya.

⑤

Destiny Laboratory Module

⑥

Canadarm2

Manufactured by the United States

Attached **February 10, 2001**

Used for scientific experiments, the Destiny lab will also serve as a docking station for all U.S. space shuttles.

Manufactured by Canada

Attached **April 22, 2001**

The robotic arm walked off its own delivery pallet and then helped unload other equipment from the space shuttle that brought it to the station.

Source: NASA (www.nasa.gov)

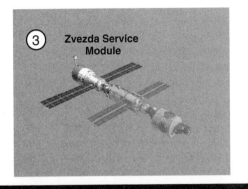

③ Zvezda Service Module

Manufactured by Russia
Attached **July 25, 2000**

Zvezda's connection to Zarya was completely automated and performed by Russian ground control.

④ Integrated Truss Structure and Solar Arrays

Manufactured by the United States
Attached **December 3, 2000**

With these additions, the space station became powered by solar energy using a system of large solar panels and batteries.

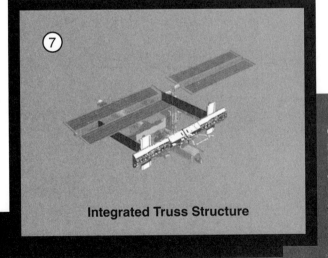

⑦ Integrated Truss Structure

Other space station missions delivered interior racks, construction materials and tools, and added connectors or other parts needed to attach the major modules.

Manufactured by the United States
Attached **April, October, and November 2002**

About 300 feet long when fully assembled, this truss creates a base for the robotic arm to travel along.

two by adjusting the amount of oxygen and other gases in the modules until they were at the same levels. Then with its remaining propulsion equipment removed, the Soyuz rocket reached a safe distance away from the station, and then fired its thrusters and burned up in Earth's atmosphere upon reentry.

In December 2000 the final piece of the ISS backbone, known as the Integrated Truss Structure, left its factory in Houston for the Kennedy Space Center. The delivery of these truss segments meant that virtually all of the United States' core structural components had left their factories and were either in orbit or being readied for launch. When the final truss segment was attached, it would mark the home stretch of the station's assembly.

These trusses were flown into orbit in October and November 2001, aboard two separate shuttle missions. The three trusses were attached with the help of the Canadarm 2 and astronauts performing space walks, and they were the last ISS components installed on the station as of the end of 2004.

With the installation of these trusses, construction of the ISS had reached a stopping point. While the future of the station was unclear, it was still an impressive achievement at its present configuration: 146 feet (44.5m) long from the Destiny lab to the Zvezda module, 240 feet (73.15m) wide across its solar arrays, and 90 feet (27.43m) high. Astronauts spent 338 hours and 17 minutes on space walks at the ISS during its construction, and the construction and maintenance of the ISS had required a total of forty-two separate space flights.

The ISS remained in orbit above Earth, and when its active construction ceased, it was an important scientific laboratory in space. While the initial components of the station were in place, it would require a constant human presence to keep the lights on while the station's future was determined.

KEEPING THE LIGHTS BURNING

On February 1, 2003, the space shuttle *Columbia* was destroyed upon reentry to Earth's atmosphere. With its loss and the subsequent investigation into the cause, the U.S. shuttle fleet was grounded, effectively leaving the ISS in limbo as well. While the station continues to be occupied by international crews consisting of astronauts from its different member countries, the future of the station itself remains in question.

KEEPING HOUSE ON THE ISS

The ISS has had a continuous human presence since 2001, and even though the grounding of the shuttles severely limited access to the station, leaving only the Russian space vehicles as a means for reaching it, it was still necessary to constantly resupply the crew of the ISS. The space station could not be left floating empty in space, because it required constant maintenance, and the scientific experiments could not be abandoned.

Although the ISS had been assembled through a series of missions that brought modules and equipment into space, the ISS crew had also been constantly monitoring, repairing, and keeping house inside the huge station from the very beginning. Even the shuttle crews who delivered the first pieces of the ISS would perform tasks intended to aid the survival of the first resident crew years in the future. After the first two phases of its construction, if the ISS were to remain successfully in operation, it would need the constant presence of a crew to keep things running smoothly.

Although the actual construction of the station itself was important, the most vital tasks performed by the ISS crews involved safety: a supply of breathable air, the removal of contaminants such as microbes and radiation, and a supply of water.

Astronauts could not survive in the ISS without a supply of oxygen, and maintaining this supply is one of the most vital

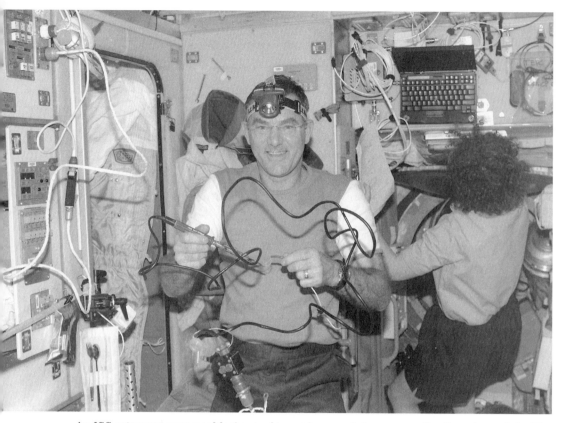

An ISS astronaut uses a soldering tool to perform maintenance on the Zvezda module. The ISS requires constant maintenance to ensure it remains in working order.

tasks performed aboard the station. Cargo vehicles that bring supplies to the station regularly deliver air, and a Russian Elektron generator aboard the Zvezda module also produces air. The Elektron produces hydrogen and oxygen by using wastewater from condensation and urine. The waste hydrogen gas, which is potentially explosive, is dumped overboard. The Elektron was not used in the ISS until several weeks after the first crew arrived, because it consumed a tremendous amount of power. Once a shuttle crew in November of 2000 installed the new solar arrays that would generate power for the ISS, the Elektron could run continuously.

Waste carbon dioxide is removed from the ISS atmosphere by the Russian Vozdukh System, which scrubs the carbon dioxide from the air and releases it overboard. Exposure to too much carbon dioxide causes severe headaches in humans. A system similar to the Russian Vozdukh System fitted inside the Destiny module had a malfunctioning vent that did not allow enough carbon dioxide to be removed from the module, causing acute headaches for the second ISS crew.

Regulating and repairing the oxygen systems aboard the ISS, as well as receiving and using fresh air tanks as they are brought up from Earth, are the most important tasks the crew carries out.

OTHER ENVIRONMENTAL CONCERNS

The ISS crew work to ensure that the environment on the station remains free from contaminants by monitoring the air processing

An astronaut works on Zvezda's Elektron oxygen generator. Powered by the space station's solar arrays, the Elektron produces oxygen from wastewater and urine.

and filtering systems aboard the station. As a result of this strict monitoring, the levels of airborne contaminants on the ISS are actually less than those found in most modern office buildings. Even the smallest spill or leak of hazardous substances can be a disaster in space, where it is not possible to open the window to let fresh air in. Because human astronauts have an unreliable sense of smell, NASA is even developing a small electronic nose to help in detecting unusual odors, according to Bond:

> A small electronic nose—about the size of a large paperback [book] . . . will be able to measure changes in humidity and monitor the most common airborne contaminants to be found on the Space Station. "Space crews are very, very busy," said Amy Ryan, principal investigator for E-Nose at the Jet Propulsion Laboratory in California. "Anything we can do to automate their tasks and keep the space habitat safe is highly desirable. Now we need to further develop the E-Nose's capability to detect various odors and differentiate between those that signify danger and those that do not."[31]

Even minor leaks of air and water cannot be ignored in a space environment. Liquid droplets from spills will float around the station and may get into the electrical systems and cause a short circuit. When the ISS crew installed the Quest airlock in July 2001, it took a half day to clean up a minor water spill safely, putting the installation of the airlock behind schedule.

On such a large and complex structure as the ISS, minor breakdowns and malfunctions will happen frequently. Although all systems are monitored continuously from the flight control centers on Earth and the ISS crew can call on technicians and former astronauts for advice, there are no specialists or mechanics on board and the crew must be able to fill these roles in maintaining and repairing their equipment, even if they have not been specifically trained for these tasks.

The crew must also manage the storage of equipment and supplies. All of the cargo brought to the ISS by the supply vehicles must be unloaded and stowed in the station in such a way that it can be found again when needed. The ISS has a computerized inventory system, but it does not always work perfectly and sometimes the crew members are left with bags of equipment that have no identifiable purpose. Waste materials and old hardware must also be stored until it can be loaded back onto a cargo vehicle and returned to Earth.

HOME REPAIR IN SPACE

In addition to the ISS crew's life support and housekeeping duties, there is also the vital job of constructing and repairing the

A CLUTTERED SPACE CLOSET

After the loss of the space shuttle *Columbia* in 2003, the number of cargo ships that visited the ISS was greatly reduced. While the crew members were still receiving the vital supplies of oxygen and other necessities from the Russian spacecraft that came to the station, for the most part these ships were unmanned vehicles that would be incinerated upon returning to Earth's atmosphere and consequently could not return things safely to Earth. The regular Russian Soyuz capsules that can return to Earth have little room for anything besides the astronauts themselves. This has left the ISS with a buildup of space clutter, such as racks of science experiments, worn-out space-walking suits, broken equipment, IMAX film, and personal belongings. While this clutter is not useful aboard the ISS, NASA does not want it to be discarded.

Shuttle deliveries and pickups have not yet been scheduled to resume, and hurricane damage to the Kennedy Space Center in 2004 also postponed the use of that facility. Meanwhile, the discarded stuff piles up inside the ISS much like a messy closet or cluttered attic.

Astronaut Ken Bowersox remarked in the 2004 Associated Press article "Space's Big Problem at International Station," that "it's at the point where we have to figure out a way to handle it. You can't just wish it away. The garbage man isn't coming tomorrow to take everything away for you."

Astronauts once routinely dumped unwanted items overboard, especially during the years of the Mir space station. This is discouraged now, since these items could become dangerous pieces of floating space debris.

An astronaut attaches thermal blankets to protect parts of the ISS's solar array system. Many ISS repairs can only be performed by humans during space walks.

ISS itself. During the first two phases of the ISS construction, astronauts from the shuttle crews and the ISS itself performed fifty-six space walks, some as long as seven hours. During these space walks, officially called extravehicular activities or EVAs, astronauts helped to attach new modules and equipment to the ISS exterior and deployed antennas, solar arrays, and gyroscopes, which help the ISS maintain its correct tilt. Although the robotic arms can accomplish the larger tasks, humans are essential for completing the fine details of construction. For example, during a typical space walk in October 2001, Russian astronaut Tyurin Dezhurov spent four hours and fifty-eight minutes attaching telemetry (long-distance communication links) and data cables between Pirs and Zvezda, and installing handrails, an access ladder, a cargo crane, a docking target, and an automated navigational antenna. Repair and maintenance tasks, such as removing debris from a docking interface and installing thermal blankets over sensitive machinery, are also performed during space walks.

Repairing and maintaining the ISS became more dangerous after the grounding of the U.S. shuttle fleet, when the number of crew members on board was reduced to two to better accommodate the smaller Russian vehicles. NASA prefers to have a crew member remain inside the ISS when a space walk takes place, but this was a luxury they could not afford during a September 2004 space walk:

> Leaving their orbital outpost unmanned, the international space station's two astronauts floated outside on a space walk and plugged in new antennas and replaced a worn-out piece of cooling equipment. "Be careful," Mission Control repeatedly warned the space walkers. Because no one was left inside the . . . complex, flight controllers in both Moscow and Houston kept close watch over the two men and all systems. The space walk lasted 5½ hours, and everything was accomplished. This was the fifth space walk with an empty outpost.[32]

DEALING WITH SPACE JUNK

Another key job for the ISS crew is monitoring and repairing damage caused by orbiting space junk. The ISS circles the earth at an altitude of 247 miles (397.51km), which is one of the most congested areas of space because of floating space junk, or debris. According to space writer Leonard David:

> Since the first satellite was hurtled spaceward in 1957 . . .
> all manner of spacecraft from numbers of nations have
> plowed their way into the heavens. From paint chips
> and lens covers to discarded space reactors and spent
> rocket stages, after four decades of heaving [these]
> satellites into Earth orbit, space has become a polluted
> junkyard.[33]

The United States' monitoring system, NORAD (North American Aerospace Defense Command) currently keeps track of more than six thousand objects in low Earth orbit that are more than 4 inches (10cm) across in size. But there are hundreds of thousands of smaller pieces that cannot be tracked. Some of this debris is destroyed naturally when Earth's atmosphere expands and the objects reenter and burn up.

In addition to the space debris generated by humans' activities in space, there are also tiny particles of dust called meteoroids, which may travel at speeds of more than 40 miles (64.37km) an hour. Even a tiny particle can cause considerable damage at that speed.

All of this space debris creates a hazard to both the ISS and the space support vehicles. Windows and solar arrays on the ISS have been pitted and scarred, and heat tiles on the shuttles have been damaged. Although some ISS modules have been constructed with shielding to protect them from space debris, the Zarya and Zvezda modules have not, and they must be constantly monitored for damage. In the future, ISS crews will most likely have to install additional shielding on these modules, as well as metal covers to protect windows that are not as thick as those on the American-built modules.

The exterior and interior of the ISS can also suffer from the constant barrage of cosmic radiation. This is radiation that is created by the sun in the form of ultraviolet light and X-rays, and it can damage solar cells, resulting in a loss of power output. It can also degrade computer chips, causing errors in the machines' memory.

The resident crew must carry out all of the construction, maintenance, and repair tasks of the ISS in order to keep the sta-

An astronaut practices using the space station's robotic arm. Before they can join the ISS program, astronauts must undergo a rigorous training regimen.

tion running successfully. This enormous responsibility requires a high degree of cooperation among the constant rotation of astronauts from the many different countries involved in its construction, including the United States, Russia, the nations of the European Space Agency, Japan, and Canada. It is a challenge to ensure that all astronauts receive the same training for life in the ISS, and that they can get along in close quarters for months at a time despite differences in language and everyday habits.

THE *COLUMBIA* TRAGEDY

One of the biggest setbacks to the continued construction of the ISS was also a great personal tragedy involving the loss of seven astronauts. On February 1, 2003, the space shuttle *Columbia* disintegrated during reentry into Earth's atmosphere, fifteen minutes before its scheduled landing at Kennedy Space Center in Florida. Eyewitnesses spoke of seeing flecks or pieces coming off the shuttle, and a sound like reverberating thunder that lasted for several minutes. Heat-sensing radar recorded a bright red streak moving through the sky.

Debris from the *Columbia* was scattered across Texas, Louisiana, and Arkansas, and human remains were found in a field in Texas later that same day.

President George W. Bush made an address to the nation shortly after the tragedy took place, saying:

> This day has brought terrible news and great sadness to our country. The *Columbia*'s lost. There are no survivors. These men and women assumed great risk in this service to all humanity. [They] knew the dangers and they faced them willingly, knowing they had a high and noble purpose in life. Because of their courage and idealism, we will miss them all the more.

The loss of the *Columbia* grounded the shuttle fleet until NASA could determine the exact cause of the accident, leaving two astronauts and a cosmonaut aboard the ISS. Transportation to the ISS was taken over by Russian spacecraft, and the U.S. shuttle fleet had not yet returned to service as of the end of 2004.

THE ISS BUS

The biggest challenge to continued habitation of the ISS came with the grounding of the U.S. shuttle fleet after the loss of the shuttle *Columbia*. The crews of the ISS had been relying on the shuttle fleet to transport astronauts and supplies to and from the station, and once the fleet became unavailable, they were forced to rely on the Russian spacecraft to accomplish these missions. Russia, suffering from financial difficulties in its own space program, began to protest this heavy reliance on their equipment, according to a 2004 article on the Space Daily Web site:

Russia will ask the United States to contribute more toward the costs of flying US astronauts to the International Space Station, a spokesman for the Russian space agency said. . . . Since the US space shuttles stopped supplying the jointly manned station in the wake of the February 2003 Columbia disaster Russia has been shouldering the burden. Space Agency Chief Antoly Perminov said earlier this week that "we shall bring the American astronauts to the ISS on a commercial basis in 2006. We accepted a temporary barter scheme for the operation of the ISS in 2005. The US writes off Russian debts for man-hours while Russia carries astronauts by Soyuz ships for free."[34]

The United States is also responsible for the construction of an ISS emergency evacuation vehicle, but severe budget cuts at NASA have delayed construction. This vehicle would be able to hold six astronauts and evacuate them from the space station in the event of a major emergency, but until the vehicle is built the ISS cannot keep a full crew on board. The temporary solution proposed by the Russians would be for NASA to purchase two Soyuz spacecraft that could be permanently docked at the ISS. Two Soyuz would be required since a ship cannot be docked for more than six months at a time before it must be brought back to Earth and replaced with a fresh vehicle.

The current difficulties with transportation to and from the ISS and the budget cuts that both the Russian and United States ISS programs are facing have led some to wonder if the ISS project should be scrapped.

A FUTURE FOR THE ISS?

The enormous construction cost of the ISS, which is still not completed, has forced the United States and Russia to take a hard look at their continued involvement in the program. As early as September 2002, the Russian Space Agency was discussing the possibility of temporarily suspending the station's construction, citing a lack of funding. In 2004 President George W. Bush announced that the increasing costs of the ISS would have to be paid for through a reduction in other areas of NASA's budget. He advocated shifting the focus of America's space exploration from the ISS to returning to the moon and exploring Mars and perhaps even Pluto.

Bush's announcement cast doubt over the ISS's future, according to a January 22, 2004 Associated Press article:

> U.S. President George Bush's vision of astronauts on the moon and Mars dims the spotlight on the international space station, leaving its long-term future murky. NASA will support the floating research lab for at least another dozen years. But beyond that, the level of U.S. support is unclear. Also unknown is whether its international partners will hang on if NASA drops out or whether the space station will be allowed to fall back to earth like Skylab did in 1979. One thing is certain. With NASA's new space exploration goal, the half-completed space station goes from being the cornerstone of the U.S. space program to merely a stepping stone for further ambitions, NASA officials and experts say.[35]

Bush's announcement, however, came at a time when the European Space Agency was readying its next two major contributions to the ISS, the Columbus Orbital Research Facility and an automated transfer vehicle for bringing supplies to the ISS. The Columbus module is scheduled to be sent into space in 2005 for assembly. The ESA is also planning to construct two more linking nodes for station components, as well as the Cupola that will provide a view of the entire ISS. The Japanese are also planning to build and launch their own scientific module, called Kibo.

The biggest arguments against the ISS concern its enormous cost, already rising above the intended $100 billion, but the annual $2.1 billion a year for the United States' contribution works out to only 2.2 cents per person in the United States per day, or about eight dollars a year. While the renewed focus on exploring Mars and beyond would seem to lead space travel away from the ISS, the station could provide a platform for launching further exploration. As John Uri, lead scientist at the Johnson Space Center, notes,

> One of the advantages of space station research is the flexibility to continue long-duration research over several expeditions, modifying research procedures and parameters to take advantage of intriguing results. We want science on the station to be as much like science in

Two future ISS modules, including the Japanese Kibo node (upper right), await launch at the Kennedy Space Center. Rising costs have significantly delayed the ISS's scheduled completion.

an Earth-based laboratory as possible, but of course without gravity.[36]

Scientists feel that the opportunity to conduct research on the ISS could result in important advances in medicine, as well as a better understanding of the effects of microgravity on physical, chemical, and biological processes. Understanding how microgravity affects the human body will aid in the future exploration and colonization of space. The ISS is also the best platform for viewing Earth, as well as studying the atmosphere, the sun, and the other planets.

Opponents of the ISS call the station a major drain on NASA's science program, forcing it to cancel some scientific missions and transfer funds from science programs to manned spaceflight. James Van Allen, a University of Iowa professor and scientist, says:

> The cost of the space station is far beyond any justifiable scientific purpose or any justifiable practical purpose. Some experiments one would like to carry out in space require highly stable platforms and the accurate aiming of scientific instruments, and so they must be free of vibrations and accelerations. An astronaut's sneeze could wreck a sensitive instrument in a microgravitational field: clouds of gas or droplets from thrusters of the spacecraft or from dumps of water or urine ruin the local vacuum and optical observation conditions, and complex

This detailed photo of Hurricane Frances was taken in August 2004 by an astronaut aboard the International Space Station.

magnetic and electric fields associated with manned spacecraft preclude certain kinds of radio observations.[37]

The future of the ISS remains uncertain, although it is scheduled to be completed as originally planned by 2010. In the meantime, there have been some attempts at involving private business in the fate of the ISS.

A HOTEL IN SPACE

In late 1999 the Russian Space Agency, in an attempt to gain private funding to offset its financial difficulties, announced that it would enter into an agreement with a company named Spacehab, which would build a privately owned and operated module for the ISS. Spacehab is a private company dedicated to supporting people who live and work in space by providing commercial space services such as research and development of equipment, engineering and analysis, payload processing and delivery, and space education and retail products. Spacehab was responsible for the operation of several cargo and research equipment carriers that have flown on shuttle resupply missions to the ISS.

Named Enterprise, the Spacehab module would be a private studio for live television and Internet broadcasts, as well as a private research area and possible accommodation for space tourism. Later, Enterprise was planned as a substitute for the United States' habitation module, which had been cancelled due to lack of funding. Spacehab officials eagerly offered to build more sleeping space and life support systems on Enterprise, which could then be used as a space hotel and bring in revenue for the ISS. Enterprise has not yet been completed or launched.

Other companies have announced intentions to build smaller space stations that would be privately operated. The Manned Commercial Space Exploration Company, known as Mircorp, is exploring the possibility of building a small private space station that could accommodate three visitors, two of whom would be paying guests. Mircorp feels that while the ISS is dedicated to science and belongs to multiple governments, there is also a market for space tourists, commercial scientists, filmmakers, and other people who might wish to visit space.

It is also likely that China will launch a space station at some point in the future, as its activities in space grow. This project

KEEPING TRACK OF EQUIPMENT

One of the biggest challenges during the early stages of ISS construction was keeping track of the continuous stream of equipment and supplies being delivered to the station on a regular basis. The computerized inventory system often did not work at all, and many hours were wasted looking for misplaced equipment or dealing with bar-coded packages with unknown purposes. The ISS log entry for January 2, 2001, demonstrates some of this frustration, as quoted in Peter Bond's book, *The Continuing Story of the International Space Station:*

> One of the bags stowed is a non-standard white bag with a paper tag on it 'ECOMM HARDWARE'. No bar code. No serial number on the bag, but there is a NASA part number. Inside the bag [is] a power cable. Cable has a label, but no bar code. Search for the bag's part number in the database—not found. Search for the cable in the database to find some more clues as to what this bag is. About six like cables turn up. Serial number for this cable says it is located in . . . definitely not the same bag [we are] holding. Pull up the history of changes, and it has been moved, moved again, and deleted on the same day, and then duplicated and added back to the database, all done by the ground, and all, we think, talking about the "wrong" bag and generating data that at best is confusing.
>
> Keeping track of equipment is just one of the challenges that the ISS crew faced in trying to construct a space station while in orbit hundreds of miles above the earth, and out of reach of the nearest hardware store.

has been discussed for more than ten years but still exists only on paper. There is also the possibility that the Chinese may join the ISS program.

All of these commercial possibilities may lead to neighbors in space for the ISS, even though its own future is uncertain at this point. The ISS was not built to last indefinitely, however, and even if construction continues and the space station is in active use, a time will come when it has to be decommissioned.

THE END OF THE ISS

Although the ISS has not yet been completed, many of its components have limited life spans due to the harsh conditions of space. Consequently, the ISS is expected to have only a ten- to fifteen-year operational life span. NASA officials know from their experiences with Skylab and the Russian experiences with Mir that they must have a plan for the eventual deconstruction of the ISS.

NASA has determined that an uncontrolled reentry of the ISS into Earth's atmosphere would pose an unacceptable threat to human life. Possible alternatives to letting the station fall to Earth would be boosting it into a higher orbit to prolong its lifetime in space, disassembling the pieces and bringing them back to Earth on the shuttle, or attempting to perform a controlled reentry with the station splashing down in the Pacific Ocean. Boosting the ISS into a higher orbit would only postpone the problem of its disposal. Disassembling it would be difficult because it was not designed to be taken apart, leaving only the option of carefully bringing the station down to Earth in a controlled manner. Mir was successfully brought back to Earth by this method, but the ISS is considerably larger and more irregularly shaped, so it would be very hard to predict its behavior once it entered Earth's atmosphere. Whenever the ISS must be dealt with, it will no doubt create a great deal of international controversy.

A BRIGHT SPOT IN THE SKY

Meanwhile, the ISS continues to orbit above Earth. It is one of the most visible objects in the night sky, and can often be seen following a west-to-east path as it appears over the western horizon and then disappears over the eastern horizon just a few minutes later.

No matter what its ultimate fate, the ISS has been an amazing series of "firsts," including the first time a partnership of nations owned and operated a space station, the first time the United States and Russia cooperated in their space technology, and even the first time one robot handed over a piece of equipment to another robot in space.

The International Space Station orbits Earth as sunlight reflects off its solar arrays. Whatever its ultimate fate, the ISS serves as a powerful symbol of international achievement in space exploration.

As NASA space station program manager Tommy Holloway said during a celebration at the Johnson Space Center commemorating forty years of human spaceflight:

> When the world looks back on the International Space Station, they will see one huge team accomplishing an incredible mission. And through integrity, trust and respecting people, no obstacle, whether technical or cultural, is preventing this world space flight team from achieving our goals.[38]

NOTES

Introduction: A Joint Venture

1. Edward Everett Hale, *The Brick Moon*, www.readbookon line.net/readOnLine/2108.

2. Peter Bond, *The Continuing Story of the International Space Station.* New York: Springer-Verlag, 2002, p. 22.

3. Quoted in Bond, *The Continuing Story of the International Space Station*, p. 26.

4. Bond, *The Continuing Story of the International Space Station*, p. xvii.

Chapter 1: The First Space Stations

5. Facts On File News Services, "From the Archives (1940–1979): USSR Launches 'Sputnik,'" October 9, 1957, www.2facts.com/Ancillaries/temp/46276temph00506.asp.

6. John F. Kennedy, State of the Union Address, May 31, 1961, www.c-span.org/executive/transcipt.asp?cat=current_event &code=bush_admin&year=1961.

7. Bond, *The Continuing Story of the International Space Station*, p. 35.

8. Piers Bizony, *Island in the Sky: Building the International Space Station.* London: Aurum Press, 1996, p. 36.

9. Ronald Reagan, Address to the Nation on Defense and National Security, March 23, 1983, www.cnn.com/SPECIALS/ cold.war/episodes/22/documents/starwars.speech.

10. Ronald Reagan, State of the Union Address, January 25, 1984, http://history.nasa.gov/reagan84.htm.

Chapter 2: Designing an International Space Station

11. Facts On File News Services, "From the Archives (1940–present): Space: U.S., Russia Set Joint Venture," September 16, 1993, www.2facts.com/stories/temp/71028temp199305 4789.asp.

12. Quoted in Bond, *The Continuing Story of the International Space Station*, p. 123.

13. Quoted in Bond, *The Continuing Story of the International Space Station*, p. 100.

14. Quoted in Bond, *The Continuing Story of the International Space Station*, p. 127.

Chapter 3: Prefabricating a Space Station

15. Quoted in David M. Harland and John E. Catchpole, *Creating the International Space Station.* New York: Springer-Verlag, 2002, p. 196.

16. Quoted in Harland and Catchpole, *Creating the International Space Station*, p. 199.

17. Space and Tech.com, "ISS Destiny (U.S. Laboratory Module)—Summary," 2001, www.spaceandtech.com/spacedata/platforms/iss-destiny_sum.shtml.

18. National Aeronautics and Space Administration, "The Amazing Canadarm2," Science@NASA, April 18, 2001, http://science.nasa.gov/headlines/y2001/ast18apr_1.htm.

19. National Aeronautics and Space Administration, "The Amazing Canadarm2."

20. SpaceRef.com, "Space Station User's Guide: ISS Elements: Joint Airlock 'Quest,'" www.spaceref.com/iss/elements/airlock.html.

21. Quoted in Kyle Herring, "Final Major ISS Segments Head to Launch Site," Radio Amateur Satellite Group, December 5, 2002, www.amsat.org/amsat/archive/sarex/200212/msg00026.html.

Chapter 4: A Construction Site in Space

22. Bond, *The Continuing Story of the International Space Station*, pp. 67–70.

23. Quoted in Bond, *The Continuing Story of the International Space Station*, p. 92.

24. National Aeronautics and Space Administration, "International Space Station Assembly: A Construction Site in Orbit," June 1999, http://spaceflight.nasa.gov/spacenews/factsheets/pdfs/assembly.pdf.

25. CNN.com, "First Space Station Segment Orbiting Smoothly," November 20, 1998, www.cnn.com/TECH/space/9811/20/station.launch.wrap01/.

26. Quoted in Harland and Catchpole, *Creating the International Space Station*, p. 210.

27. Quoted in Anatoly Zak, "Zvezda En Route to Space Station," Space.com, July 12, 2000, www.space.com/missionlaunches/launches/zvezda_launch_000712.html.

28. Quoted in Bond, *The Continuing Story of the International Space Station*, p. 181.

29. Quoted in Bond, *The Continuing Story of the International Space Station*, p. 183.

30. Quoted in Bond, *The Continuing Story of the International Space Station*.

Chapter 5: Keeping the Lights Burning

31. Bond, *The Continuing Story of the International Space Station*, p. 241.

32. Marcia Dunn, "Spacewalking Astronauts Replace Worn-Out Piece of Cooling Equipment," Associated Press, September 4, 2004, www.nctimes.com/articles/2004/09/04/special_reports/science_technology/18_15_359_3_04.txt.

33. Leonard David, "When What Goes Up Comes Down," Space.com, September 6, 2000, www.space.com/science astronomy/planetearth/space_debris_000905.html.

34. Space Daily, "Russia Wants US to Pay for Astronaut Flights to Space Station," December 30, 2004, www.spacedaily. com/2004/041230102255.jzqrpfv5.html.

35. Associated Press, "Moon, Mars Plans Put Space Station in Doubt," January 22, 2004, www.ctv.ca/servlet/ArticleNews/story/CTVNews/1074777978139_19?s_name=&no_ads=.

36. Quoted in Bond, *The Continuing Story of the International Space Station*, p. 275.

37. Quoted in Bond, *The Continuing Story of the International Space Station*, p. 279.

38. Johnson Space Center, "JSC Celebrates 40 Years of Human Space Flight," http://www.jsc.nasa.gov/history/jsc40/jsc40_pg19.htm.

FOR FURTHER READING

Books

James Barter, *Space Stations*. San Diego, CA: Lucent Books, 2004. A look at the space stations that have orbited Earth, as well as the living conditions and the experiments that take place in them.

Henry M. Holden, *Living and Working Aboard the International Space Station*. Berkeley Heights, NJ: MyReportLinks.com Books, 2004. An excellent sourcebook with many links to Web sites about the International Space Station.

Roger D. Launius, *Space Stations: Base Camps to the Stars*. Washington, DC: Smithsonian Books, 2003. A well-illustrated look at space stations from their origins to the ISS, written by a former NASA chief historian.

Dew Nipaul, *The International Space Station: An Orbiting Laboratory*. New York: Children's Press, 2004. A good look at the ISS and its purpose as a laboratory for scientific experimentation.

Elaine Pascoe, *The International Space Station*. San Diego, CA: Blackbirch Press, 2003. Focuses on the construction of the ISS and the many dangers the astronauts face, as well as the benefits that will result.

Web Sites

How Stuff Works: How Space Stations Work (www.howstuff works.com/space-station.htm). A look at space stations, how they work, and how they are built.

National Aeronautics and Space Administration (NASA): International Space Station (http://spaceflight.nasa.gov/station/index.html). NASA's Web site about the ISS, with activities and links to every aspect of the station, as well as a link that allows you to track its current location.

PBS: *Space Station: A Rare Inside View of the Next Frontier in Space Exploration* (www.pbs.org/spacestation). A companion site to the PBS special about the ISS, with opportunities to explore the station and learn about its purpose.

WORKS CONSULTED

Books

Piers Bizony, *Island in the Sky: Building the International Space Station.* London: Aurum Press, 1996. An older book that takes a good look at the space stations built before the ISS and the plans for the new international space station.

Peter Bond, *The Continuing Story of the International Space Station.* New York: Springer-Verlag, 2002. An excellent overall look at the construction of the ISS and the stations that came before it, as well as what life is like on board.

W. David Compton and Charles D. Benson, *Living and Working in Space: A History of Skylab.* Washington, DC: U.S. Government Printing Office, 1983. A comprehensive book about America's first space station, Skylab, as well as a behind-the-scenes look at NASA.

Joy Hakim, *A History of US: All the People 1945–1998*, 2nd ed. New York: Oxford University Press, 1999. An excellent look at the politics and events of United States history, including the Cold War and the early space race.

Edward Everett Hale, *The Brick Moon.* Whitefish, MT: Kessinger Publishing, 2004. www.readbookonline.net/readOnLine/2108. Originally published in 1869, this short story was one of the first science fiction stories about the possibility of life on an artificial structure in space.

David M. Harland, *The Mir Space Station: A Precursor to Space Colonization.* New York: John Wiley & Sons, 1997. This book focuses on the construction and operation of the Mir space station, with excellent photographs.

David M. Harland and John E. Catchpole, *Creating the International Space Station.* New York: Springer-Verlag, 2002. A history of the construction of the ISS, starting with the Apollo era, with detailed explanations of the orbital assembly of the station.

Internet Sources

Associated Press, "Moon, Mars Plans Put Space Station in Doubt," January 22, 2004. www.ctv.ca/servlet/ArticleNews/story/CTVNews/1074777978139_19?s_name=&no_ads=.

Associated Press, "Space's Big Problem at International Station," October 4, 2004. http://www.signonsandiego.com/uniontrib/20041004/news_1n4space.html.

CNN.com, "Bush to Families: 'Entire Nation Grieves with You,'"
    February 1, 2003. www.cnn.com/2003/US/02/01/shuttle.bush.
    statement.

CNN.com, "First Space Station Segment Orbiting Smoothly,"
    November 20, 1998. www.cnn.com/TECH/space/9811/20/
    station.launch.wrap01.

Leonard David, "When What Goes Up Comes Down," Space.
    com, September 6, 2000. www.space.com/scienceastronomy/
    planetearth/space_debris_000905.html.

Marcia Dunn, "Spacewalking Astronauts Replace Worn-Out
    Piece Of Cooling Equipment," Associated Press, September
    4, 2004. www.nctimes.com/articles/2004/09/04/special-
    reports/science_technology/18_15_359_3_04.txt.

Facts On File News Services, "From the Archives (1940–1979):
    USSR Launches 'Sputnik,'" October 9, 1957. www.2facts.
    com/Ancillaries/temp/46276temph00506.asp.

———, "From the Archives (1940–present): Space: U.S., Russia
    Set Joint Venture," September 16, 1993. www.2facts.com/
    stories/temp/71028temp1993054789.asp.

Kyle Herring, "Final Major ISS Segments Head to Launch Site,"
    Radio Amateur Satellite Group, December 5, 2002. www.
    amsat.org/amsat/archive/sarex/200212/msg00026.html.

John F. Kennedy, State of the Union Address, May 31, 1961. www.
    c-span.org/executive/transcript.asp?cat=current_event&code
    =bushadmin&year=1961.

Johnson Space Center, "JSC Celebrates 40 Years of Human
    Space Flight." www.jsc.nasa.gov/history/jsc40/jsc40_pg19.
    htm.

National Aeronautics and Space Administration, "The Amazing
    Canadarm2," Science@NASA, April 18, 2001. http://science.
    nasa.gov/headlines/y2001/ast18apr_1.htm.

———, "International Space Station Assembly: A Construction
    Site in Orbit," June 1999. http://spaceflight.nasa.gov/space
    news/factsheets/pdfs/assembly.pdf.

Ronald Reagan, Address to the Nation on Defense and National
    Security, March 23, 1983. www.cnn.com/SPECIALS/cold.
    war/episodes/22/documents/starwars.speech.

———, State of the Union Address, January 25, 1984. http://history.
    nasa.gov/reagan84.htm.

Space and Tech.com, "ISS Destiny (U.S. Laboratory Module)—Summary," 2001. www.spaceandtech.com/spacedata/platforms/iss-destiny_sum.shtml.

Space Daily, "Russia Wants US to Pay for Astronaut Flights to Space Station," December 30, 2004. www.spacedaily.com/2004/041230102255.jzqrpfv5.html.

SpaceRef.com, "Space Station User's Guide: ISS Elements: Joint Airlock 'Quest.'" www.spaceref.com/iss/elements/airlock.html.

"Space Station 3D: Film Mission: Behind the Scenes: Myers on her Orbitting Filmmakers." www.imax.com/spacestation.

Anatoly Zak, "Zvezda En Route to Space Station," Space.com, July 12, 2000. www.space.com/missionlaunches/launches/zvezda_launch_000712.html.

INDEX

PICTURE CREDITS

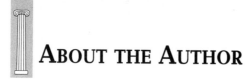

ABOUT THE AUTHOR

Marcia Amidon Lüsted has a degree in English and secondary education and has worked as an English teacher, bookseller, and musician. She lives in Hancock, New Hampshire, with her husband and three sons.